HOW TO GET OUT OF
LONDON
WITHOUT REALLY TRYING

Edited by Ben Olins & Jane Smillie

Additional research by Alex Lim

Published in 2016 by Herb Lester Associates Ltd

How To Get Out Of London Without Really Trying
Text by Ben Olins © Herb Lester Associates Ltd 2016
Cover illustration by Matt Chase © Herb Lester Associates Ltd 2016

A CIP catalogue record for this book is available from the British Library

ISBN: 978-1-910023-62-4

Printed and bound in the United Kingdom by The Westdale Press Ltd
Cover: Cocoon offset 100% recycled board
Pages: Cocoon offset 100% recycled paper

Herb Lester Associates Ltd are committed to printing and publishing in the
United Kingdom using 100% recycled materials wherever possible.

Herb Lester Associates Limited Reg. No 7183338

To see the full range of Herb Lester books, guides and products
visit herblester.com

CONTENTS

A note about using this book

All details are correct at the time of writing, but we urge you to call ahead before setting out. Admission prices are not listed, please check websites for details. Opening times listed as seasonal will change throughout the year.

Many large houses and some galleries and museums close for private events. Pub opening hours indicate when the doors open and close, food serving times may be different. Travelling times are based on fastest routes from London.

Entries are grouped into chapters by journey time from a mainline train station, with a couple of exceptions that are accessible by tube.

**LONDON IS A CITY OF INFINITE VARIETY AND TIMELESS
APPEAL, BUT SOMETIMES ALL WE WANT IS TO GET OUT.**

Considering that a journey of just a few miles across town can
take well over an hour, it's remarkable how soon after boarding
a train one can be dipping toes in chilly coastal waters or roaming
lush countryside.

We have designed this book with the needs of the impatient
city-dweller or time-strapped tourist in mind. It is for those of
us who want a quick escape with minimal effort, just a few hours
respite rather than a holiday, with no planning and no packing.
Everywhere that we've recommended is a short train journey
away. Some may require a change en route, others a bit of a walk
or a bus at the other end, but nothing should take more than two
hours from a mainline station and most will be considerably less.

Our determination to keep travel time to under two hours by public
transport created tough decisions, some favourite places are just a
shade too distant or an unrealistic option without a vehicle. What
we are left with is a fantastic array that should offer something for
everyone, regardless of mood, interests or time restrictions.

It is our hope that this book inspires many happy days, mornings
and afternoons out.

Ben Olins & Jane Smillie
London, June 2016

UNDER 30 MINUTES

BEKONSCOT MODEL VILLAGE

HARLOW'S PUBLIC ART

HATFIELD HOUSE

LIGHTBOX GALLERY

RAF MUSEUM

RED HOUSE

BEKONSCOT MODEL VILLAGE

THE WORLD'S OLDEST MODEL VILLAGE, opened in the late 1920s, still seems redolent of more innocent times. There are no binge-drinkers here, nor out of town shopping centres, instead the visitor follows a path that passes towns and villages with greens and thriving high streets, farms, grand houses, quarry, circus, zoo — there's even a fire brigade, hard at work extinguishing a blaze in a thatched roof. A tiny railway calls at stations across the landscape, dwarfed by shrubs that line the track. Another larger railway transports visitors around the village's perimeter. A picnic area is thankfully full size, as are the refreshments served in the tea room.

. . . .

WARWICK ROAD, BEACONSFIELD, BUCKINGHAMSHIRE HP9 2PL / TEL: 01494 672919
SEASONAL OPENING, February to November
MARYLEBONE TO BEACONSFIELD, *approx 7 minute walk* / **JOURNEY TIME** 30 minutes

HARLOW'S PUBLIC ART

THERE ARE 84 PIECES OF PUBLIC ART dotted across this postwar new town. An early Barbara Hepworth is positioned on a housing estate, Lynn Chadwick's Trigon in a shopping precinct, Elizabeth Frink's Boar stands in a pool in front of the civic centre, inside which is Henry Moore's Harlow Family Group. The civic centre is also home to The Gibberd Gallery, which oversees the town's sculpture collection and has an exhibition space in its own right.

A map of Harlow's sculpture can be downloaded from visitessex.com or pick one up at The Gibberd Gallery.

GIBBERD GALLERY CIVIC CENTRE, THE WATER GARDENS, HARLOW, ESSEX CM20 1WG / TEL: 01279 446404
MON-FRI: *9am-4.45pm*
LIVERPOOL STREET TO HARLOW TOWN/ **JOURNEY TIME** 30 minutes

HATFIELD HOUSE

MUCH MORE THAN JUST a house (vast, Jacobean), it's also a palace (substantial, Tudor), gardens (large) and park (huge). Hatfield House is the "new" part, completed in 1611 by Robert Cecil, first Earl of Salisbury, whose heirs still live a short walk away in the old palace, where Elizabeth I spent much of her childhood. The House contains the Virgin Queen's Rainbow portrait and other items associated with her, along with all the accoutrements of a great family: arms, armour, many important paintings and tapestries. Tucked away behind the Old Palace are a restaurant and shops. Call before visiting, parts of the house and grounds may be closed for weddings or private functions.

HATFIELD, HERTFORDSHIRE AL9 5NQ / TEL: 01707 287010
OPENING HOURS FOR HOUSE AND GARDENS VARY, call for details
KING'S CROSS TO HATFIELD / **JOURNEY TIME** 25 minutes

LIGHTBOX GALLERY

IT'S WORTH CHECKING what's on at this modest modern gallery, which contains three exhibition spaces as well as a local history museum. British art of the 20th century is the main focus, with a strong collection that includes paintings and sculpture by Edward Burra, John Craxton, John Tunnard, Elisabeth Frink, Sir Jacob Epstein, Eric Gill, Barbara Hepworth, Lynn Chadwick and Eduardo Paolozzi. In summer the pretty, leafy canalside setting is particularly pleasant, with the café making full use of outside seating.

....

CHOBHAM ROAD, WOKING, SURREY GU21 4AA / TEL: 01483 737800
TUE-SAT: *10.30am-5pm*; SUN: *11am-4pm*
WATERLOO TO WOKING, *approx 5 minute walk* / **JOURNEY TIME** 30 MINS

RAF MUSEUM

NEITHER THE APPROACH FROM COLINDALE tube station nor the museum's exterior offers much promise, which makes being inside that much more of a surprise. The sheer scale of many of the planes is quite overwhelming. Legendary names such as the Sopwith Camel and Spitfire are represented, as are examples from Japan, Germany, Russia and America. Almost as much a museum of flight as of conflict, it encompasses the first, flimsiest gliders up to the high-tech machines of present day.

....

GRAHAME PARK WAY, HENDON, LONDON NW9 5LL / TEL: 020 8205 2266
DAILY: *10am-5.30pm*
CHARING CROSS UNDERGROUND TO COLINDALE (NORTHERN LINE), *approx 10 minute walk* / **JOURNEY TIME** 30 minutes

RED HOUSE

WHEN THIS HOUSE WAS BUILT for William Morris in 1860 the area was semi-rural Kent. Today it's just another outer London suburb, but the house and grounds still have an air of the countryside about them, and the outdoor café and garden are a joyous sight. Designed in the Arts and Crafts style to plans by Morris and architect Philip Webb, it's a merry building — L-shaped, with windows in all shapes and sizes and a great many gables. Inside it seems that every element is considered, with furniture and fittings designed for purpose and beauty.

....

RED HOUSE LANE, BEXLEYHEATH, LONDON DA6 8JF / TEL: 020 8304 9878
WED-SUN: *11am-1.30pm (tours only); 1.30pm-4.15pm*
LONDON BRIDGE TO BEXLEYHEATH, *approx 15 minute walk* / **JOURNEY TIME** 30 minutes

30-60 MINUTES

BATTLESBRIDGE ANTIQUES CENTRE

BLETCHLEY PARK

BOOKHAM COMMONS

BOX HILL

BROOKLANDS MUSEUM

CAMBRIDGE

CAPEL MANOR COLLEGE GARDENS

CHISLEHURST CAVES

CROYDON AIRPORT VISITOR CENTRE

DOWN HOUSE

ELTHAM PALACE

EPPING FOREST

EPPING ONGAR RAILWAY

FORTY HALL

HALL PLACE AND GARDENS

HAM HOUSE

HAMPTON COURT PALACE

HIGGINS BEDFORD

LEIGH-ON-SEA

MYDDELTON HOUSE GARDENS

NORSEY WOOD

RICHMOND PARK / PETERSHAM NURSERIES

RUISLIP LIDO & RAILWAY

SOUTHEND-ON-SEA

STRAWBERRY HILL

BATTLESBRIDGE ANTIQUES CENTRE

IF THE HUNT GIVES AS MUCH PLEASURE AS THE CATCH, head to this village with around 80 dealers in antiques and collectables. With so much to look at, the promise of treasure is always there, and perseverance – and a bit of luck – usually pays off. These days, the mid 20th century is best represented, with furniture, clothes, records and homeware but you'll find older items too. On Sundays, the small motorbike museum is well worth the one pound admission fee.

THE OLD GRANARY, HAWK HILL, BATTLESBRIDGE, ESSEX SS11 7RE / TEL: 01268 769000
DAILY: *10am-5pm*
LIVERPOOL STREET TO BATTLESBRIDGE / **JOURNEY TIME** 45 minutes

BLETCHLEY PARK

TOP SECRET HQ of Britain's World War Two codebreakers is now firmly on the map as a tourist destination. Exhibits are arranged across the main house and the huts in which Alan Turing and colleagues laboured. Considerable expense has gone into turning this into a visitor experience, making it popular with families and fans of The Imitation Game. Tickets last for a year with any number of return visits. Not included is entry to The National Museum of Computing and the National Radio Centre, both in the grounds.

THE MANSION, BLETCHLEY PARK, SHERWOOD DRIVE, BLETCHLEY, BUCKINGHAMSHIRE MK3 6EB / TEL: 01908 640404
NOVEMBER-FEBRUARY, DAILY: *9.30am-4pm*
MARCH-OCTOBER, DAILY: *9.30am-5pm*
EUSTON TO BLETCHLEY / **JOURNEY TIME** 40 minutes

(L) Steve Crowhurst (R) Alistair Young

BOOKHAM COMMONS

BLESSEDLY CLOSE TO THE RAILWAY STATION, these substantial ancient commons are home to a variety of wildlife, including the rare Purple Emperor butterfly. There are trails for walkers and cyclists that take into account differing energy levels, guiding the visitor through marshes, woodland, glades and past ponds.

CHURCH ROAD, GREAT BOOKHAM, SURREY KT23 3LT
WATERLOO TO BOOKHAM / **JOURNEY TIME** 50 minutes

Brooklands Museum

BOX HILL

IN THE SURREY HILLS on the North Downs, this is an idyllic spot for kite-flying, butterfly-spotting, woodland walks and picnics (as in Jane Austen's Emma "every body had a burst of admiration on first arriving"). It's also a place to spot wild box trees, more commonly seen as manicured hedges. And there's Olympic-level cycling too on the Zig Zag Road, which was considered the most grueling stage of the London 2012 road race cycling event.

TADWORTH, SURREY KT20 7LB
WATERLOO TO BOX HILL & WESTHUMBLE, *approx 10 minute walk* /
JOURNEY TIME 60 minutes

BROOKLANDS MUSEUM

FOR MUCH OF THE 20TH CENTURY this was a place of motor races, speed trials and, later, a major centre for aircraft design, construction and testing. The current museum reflects all that, with displays of historic cars, motorbikes and aircraft from the earliest days to the present. Even Concorde is here, with visitors able to take a virtual flight for a small additional fee. Events, including speed trials, are still held here so it's worth checking their website for the best time to visit. Also on the grounds is the separate London Bus Museum, showing vehicles from the 19th-century horse-drawn omnibus to the recently departed Routemaster, it's an insight into a mode of transport that may not be quite as thrilling as its high-speed neighbours but is remembered with perhaps even greater affection.

BROOKLANDS ROAD, WEYBRIDGE, SURREY KT13 0QN /
TEL: 01932 857381
MARCH-OCTOBER, DAILY: *10am-5pm (last admission one hour before closing)*
NOVEMBER-FEBRUARY, DAILY: *10am-4pm (last admission one hour before closing)*
WATERLOO TO WEYBRIDGE, *approx 20 minute walk* /
JOURNEY TIME 50 minutes

The Fitzwilliam Museum

CAMBRIDGE

THE SUGGESTIONS THAT FOLLOW ARE EXCELLENT — *we wouldn't be doing our job if they weren't — even without them, a day spent aimlessly in this charming city is not one that's wasted. Its modest scale makes it eminently walkable, which means it's easy to admire lovely college buildings before wending your way to the waters of the Cam. In fact, the only down side is tearing yourself away.*

KING'S CROSS TO CAMBRIDGE / **JOURNEY TIME** 50 minutes

Fitzbillies

THE FITZWILLIAM MUSEUM

Within this monumental neo-classical structure is found 200 years'-worth of acquisitions and bequests. Egyptian relics, illuminated manuscripts, armour and weaponry, and paintings by Turner, Hogarth, Rembrandt, Canaletto, Pissarro and Monet.

TRUMPINGTON STREET, CAMBRIDGE CB2 1RB /
TEL: 01223 332900
TUE-SAT: *10am-5pm;* SUN: *12noon-5pm*

POLAR MUSEUM

Admirers of the age of adventure will be thrilled by this museum of polar exploration. Displays include journals, photographs, equipment and clothing, to vividly illustrate the unmitigated misery endured by early explorers Scott, Shackleton and those who later trod in their icy footsteps.

LENSFIELD ROAD, CAMBRIDGE CB2 1EP /
TEL: 01223 336540
TUE-SAT: *10am-4pm*

FITZBILLIES

Just like its grander namesake, another local institution in buoyant form. To outward appearance this cake shop is unchanged in 90 years — it has the original nouveau-like fascia with its distinctive script spelling out the name, even the same famously sticky Chelsea buns. It's a favourite with visitors and the more traditionally-minded student, but the sight of breakfast and lunch options such as avocado on toast, shakshuka and celeriac 'steak' announce that we're in the 21st century, which is not always a bad thing. Extremely tasty and extremely popular — there are no reservations, so expect to wait a while for a table.

51-52 TRUMPINGTON STREET,
CAMBRIDGE CB2 1RG /
TEL: 01223 352500
MON-THU: *8am-6pm;* FRI: *8am-7pm;*
SAT: *9am-7pm;* SUN: *10am-6pm*

KETTLE'S YARD

Modern and contemporary art gallery in charming residential premises, currently undergoing significant renovation to create improved exhibition galleries, a new entrance area and café. It's due to reopen in Autumn 2017.

CASTLE STREET, CAMBRIDGE CB3 0AQ / TEL: 01223 748100

UNIVERSITY ZOOLOGY MUSEUM

This hulking 1960s Brutalist edifice is a satisfying contrast to the city's prettiness. For now though we can only enjoy the exterior — a major renovation is underway, due to be unveiled in early 2017.

DOWNING STREET, CAMBRIDGE CB2 3EJ / TEL: 01223 336650

CAMBRIDGE UNIVERSITY BOTANIC GARDEN

The central location of these mature gardens adds to their charm — to find 40 acres of such diversity and beauty so close to town feels particularly special. There's year-round appeal here, even in winter there's plenty to see in the glasshouses and in the wider garden where seasonal trails guide visitors to the best displays. A newly built café with outdoor seating is a pleasant spot .

1 BROOKSIDE, CAMBRIDGE CB2 1JE / TEL: 01223 336265
NOVEMBER-JANUARY, DAILY: *10am-4pm*
FEBRUARY, MARCH & OCTOBER,
DAILY: *10am-5pm*
APRIL-SEPTEMBER, DAILY: *10am-6pm*

Kettle's Yard

ARTHUR SHEPHERD

It is disheartening to note that students at Cambridge are no better dressed than their counterparts elsewhere. This despite the presence of Arthur Shepherd, a venerable gentleman's outfitter of a type all but extinct. Here is a place where tweed, corduroy, Shetland wool and waxed cotton are the stock in trade, and if that fails to entice you, stop by anyway to enjoy the changing display of flowers atop the shop's exterior.

32 TRINITY STREET, CAMBRIDGE CB2 1TB / TEL: 01223 353962
MON-SAT: *9am-5.15pm*

CAPEL MANOR COLLEGE GARDENS

IN THE GROUNDS OF THIS COLLEGE of horticulture are a series of showcase garden designs, from practical to whimsical. Le Jardin De Vincent is an homage to Van Gogh's paintings of Provence; on Sunflower Street are seven quite different houses each given its own front and back garden; there's a Japanese garden, another in the style of the 17th century and Woodland Walk. It's not just for horticulturalists though, an Italianate maze is hard to resist and The Animal Corner has pigs, poultry, goats, rabbits and Clydesdale horses, which still work some land here.

BULLSMOOR LANE, ENFIELD, MIDDLESEX EN1 4RQ / TEL: 08456 122122
MARCH-OCTOBER, DAILY: *10am-5.30pm*
NOVEMBER-FEBRUARY, MON-FRI: *10am-5pm*
LIVERPOOL STREET TO TURKEY STREET, *approx 20 minute walk* / **JOURNEY TIME** 50 minutes

(R) Harris Digital

CHISLEHURST CAVES

GUIDED TOURS OF THIS 22-FEET NETWORK of manmade tunnels are enjoyably amateurish, making fun theatre of the dank and dark environment. The emphasis is on supernatural speculation, but the Caves' real history — wartime refuge, rock'n'roll venue in the 1960s and '70s, and a chalk and flint mine from at least the 13th century — is every bit as fascinating. The tunnels are quite spacious but claustrophobics may wish to give it a miss. Comfortable shoes are recommended.

....

CAVESIDE CLOSE, OLD HILL, CHISLEHURST, KENT BR7 5NL / TEL: 020 8467 3264
WED-SUN (AND BANK HOLIDAYS): *Guided tours only*
CHARING CROSS TO CHISLEHURST, *approx 5 minute walk* / **JOURNEY TIME** 35 minutes

CROYDON AIRPORT VISITOR CENTRE

MUCH OF LONDON'S FIRST INTERNATIONAL AIRPORT has been converted for use as offices, but its history is clearly visible, not least from the De Havilland Heron imposingly perched over the entrance. On the first Sunday of each month a group of enthusiasts open the building for tours that begin in the old booking hall (now reception), with three galleries of photographs and documents and the  old control tower, with flight simulator. All this gives ample insight into the airport's significance in the early days of flight, as a military base in both world wars, start and finish point of several record-breaking flights and the country's first international airport.

....

AIRPORT HOUSE, PURLEY WAY, CROYDON, SURREY CR0 0XZ / TEL: 07779 681035
FIRST SUNDAY OF THE MONTH, *11am-4pm. Additional open days, call for details.*
LONDON BRIDGE TO PURLEY, *approx 10 minute bus ride* / **JOURNEY TIME** 40 minutes

DOWN HOUSE

THIS LARGE, COMFORTABLE HOUSE was Charles Darwin's home, for 40 years from 1842, and still looks the part. Where possible the original furniture has been used; notably Darwin's office is largely intact, including the chair in which he sat and wrote On the Origin of Species By Means of Natural Selection. There's also a recreation of his study from the ship The Beagle, and throughout are reminders that this was home to a lively family as well as a place of work. In the grounds there's a meadow, kitchen garden, hot house with orchids and insectivorous plants, and the sandwalk around which Darwin strode three times a day, year-round, although visitors with less on their mind will find it much more pleasant in summer.

LUXTED ROAD, DOWNE, KENT BR6 7JT / TEL: 01689 859119
OPEN YEAR-ROUND, SEASONAL OPENING, call for details
CHARING CROSS TO ORPINGTON, *approx 20 minute bus ride* / **JOURNEY TIME** 45 minutes

ELTHAM PALACE

IN THE MID 1930S STEPHEN AND VIRGINIA COURTAULD took on the crumbling ruins of old Eltham Palace, adapting it for their very modern, very privileged lives — it was perhaps the ultimate fixer-upper. Throughout the building there's an extraordinary mingling of the medieval with art deco, with no luxury spared. There's a map room solely for the purpose of planning travels, billiards room in the air raid bunker, Virginia Courtauld's bathroom walls are lined with onyx, with gold mosaic tiles above the bath. Even the pet lemur had underfloor heating in his cage space — and when they went sailing he had his own deck chair too. At its heart is the 15th-century Great Hall, stylishly incorporated into a new structure, that brought jazz age parties to a place where kings once sat. With so much to see, and such an abundance of detail, the free electronic guide to the house and gardens is recommended.

COURT YARD, ELTHAM, GREENWICH, LONDON SE9 5QE / TEL: 020 8294 2548
SEASONAL OPENING, call for details
LONDON BRIDGE TO MOTTINGHAM, *approx 15 minute walk* / **JOURNEY TIME** 35 minutes

(L) English Heritage (R) Paul Smith

EPPING FOREST

THE TEMPTATION IS TO TAKE THE TUBE out to this ancient and mysterious woodland, but arriving at Chingford railway instead makes a more logical start. Begin at The View visitor centre for maps and to see Queen Elizabeth's Hunting Lodge, also used by Henry VIII, who rested his bulky frame at a first floor window from which he took shots at whatever wildlife passed into view. There are still deer in the forest, cattle too, but at almost 12 miles long and two and a half wide, don't expect to see everything.

....

(THE VIEW) 6 RANGERS ROAD, CHINGFORD, LONDON, E4 7QH / TEL: 020 8532 1010
LIVERPOOL STREET TO CHINGFORD, *approx 10 minute walk* / **JOURNEY TIME** 40 minutes

EPPING ONGAR RAILWAY

AT THE EASTERN TIP OF THE LONDON UNDERGROUND, disused sections of the line have been turned into a vintage railway attraction. A bus service using 1940s vehicles runs from Epping tube station to North Weald station, from which point steam and diesel trains leave for Ongar and Coopersale, passing through Epping Forest. At Ongar and along the way, passengers can disembark and explore, and there are additional heritage bus services around the area, all handily included in a single ticket price.

....

ONGAR STATION, STATION APPROACH, ONGAR, ESSEX CM5 9BN / TEL: 01277 365200
Call for timetable
LIVERPOOL STREET UNDERGROUND TO EPPING (CENTRAL LINE) / **JOURNEY TIME** 35 minutes

FORTY HALL

A 1720S MANOR HOUSE that's been carefully restored by Enfield Council, with possibly a little too much consideration for families — dressing up boxes and Hidden Trail Chests sit uneasily in such elegant, formal spaces. Substantial grounds include a walled garden, ornamental lake, fishing ponds dug in the 1500s and, beyond, a working farm with its own orchard and vineyard.

FORTY HILL, ENFIELD EN2 9HA / TEL: 020 8363 8196
APRIL-OCTOBER: TUE-FRI: *11am-5pm;* SAT-SUN: *12noon-5pm*
NOVEMBER-MARCH; TUE-FRI: *11am-4pm;* SAT-SUN: *12noon-4pm*
LIVERPOOL STREET TO TURKEY STREET, *approx 20 minute walk* / **JOURNEY TIME** 50 minutes

HALL PLACE AND GARDENS

BUILT IN THE 1540S and substantially added to in the next century, the house's two architectural styles are plain to see. The older side is constructed of stone from a nearby monastery, the later addition in red brick. Visitors enter through the newer wing, passing into the Tudor side with its panelled great hall and minstrel's gallery, chapel  and bell tower. But it's the gardens that are the main attraction, most notably the Queen's Beasts, topiary sculptures of heraldic statues. The River Cray winds through the grounds, in which are also a wildflower meadow, greenhouse with fishpond and separately run owl house, butterfly house and nursery.

Now owned by the local council, funding is an issue which means that the star attraction, the Great Hall, may be inaccessible when hired for events.

BOURNE ROAD, BEXLEY, KENT DA5 1PQ / TEL: 01322 526574
DAILY: *9am-dusk (*HOUSE AND VISITOR CENTRE *10am-5pm)*
LONDON BRIDGE TO BEXLEY, *approx 5 minute walk* / **JOURNEY TIME** 45 minutes

HAM HOUSE

IN THE CASE OF THIS GRAND 17TH-CENTURY HOUSE, getting there is all part of the pleasure. From Richmond Station, walk either along the Thames Path or via King Henry's Mound, from which are stirring views of the capital.

Surrounded by formal and working gardens, the house provides a compelling insight into the early residents' lives, with their many collections, imposing public rooms, elaborate carved staircase, kitchen, cellars and even a bathroom equipped with round wooden tub and bed.

HAM STREET, HAM, RICHMOND, SURREY TW10 7RS / TEL: 020 8940 1950
APRIL-SEPTEMBER, DAILY: *10am-5pm* (HOUSE *12noon-4pm)*
OCTOBER-MARCH: Seasonal opening hours apply, call for details
WATERLOO TO RICHMOND, *approx 35 minute walk* / **JOURNEY TIME** 55 minutes

HAMPTON COURT PALACE

FOR THE FULL EXPERIENCE, take a boat from Westminster — the three-and-a-half-hour trip is the route taken by the palace's earliest owners, Cardinal Wolsey (who built it) and Henry VIII (who took it from him). Even without that journey, there's too much to see in a single visit. The building is vast, the Tudor original substantially added to with an extension by Sir Christopher Wren. There are state rooms and private apartments, kitchens (including the royal chocolate kitchen), tapestries, a major art collection and acres of gardens, including the famous maze — so tall and dense it can be quite unnerving. A visit off-season is more relaxing, allowing time to explore and spot details that might otherwise pass unnoticed, such as graffiti on the King's Staircase and the entwined initials of Henry VIII and Anne Boleyn under the clock tower.

EAST MOLESEY, SURREY KT8 9AU / TEL: 08444 827777
SEASONAL OPENING, call for details
WATERLOO TO HAMPTON COURT / **JOURNEY TIME** 35 minutes

Hampton Court Palace

HIGGINS BEDFORD

THREE SEPARATE INSTITUTIONS have been brought together in a single space formed from the Victorian home of the Higgins family and the brewery that made their fortune. It's an ambitious project that's not entirely satisfactory in its implementation, but the works on show make it worth travelling to. The collections encompass fine and decorative art, social history and archaeology. Perhaps of most interest to out-of-town visitors are the significant holdings of work by Edward Bawden and William Burges, the latter a 19th-century architect and designer. Of the large number of his works on display, the Sleeping Beauty Bed and Zodiac Settle, wildly exotic painted furniture designed for his own use, are particularly startling in their extravagance. The Higgins has an archive of some 3,000 works by Bawden, donated by the artist shortly before his death.

CASTLE LANE, BEDFORD, BEDFORDSHIRE MK40 3XD / TEL: 01234 718618
TUE-SAT: *11am-5pm;* SUN: *2pm-5pm*
ST PANCRAS INTERNATIONAL TO BEDFORD, *20 minute walk* / **JOURNEY TIME** 55 minutes

LEIGH-ON-SEA

LIVING IN THE SHADOW OF SOUTHEND has been good to Leigh. With crowds drawn to its larger neighbour, this small estuary town has been able to keep its focus on sailing and fishing. This is best seen in the pubs, restaurants, fish and chip shops and cockle sheds of Old Leigh, the charming seafront side of town.

A few hundred metres up steep hills and steps is The Broadway, the town's main area for shopping and eating — try **THE SAND BAR** for keenly priced local seafood. The **CAPPUCCINO CAFE AND BAKERY** has a name that requires no further description, save that both aspects are excellent and the Lloyd Loom fittings a fine choice. **ATELIER GALLERY** displays an interesting mix of midcentury furniture at fair prices and exhibitions of painting, sculpture and printmaking.

....

FENCHURCH STREET TO LEIGH-ON-SEA / **JOURNEY TIME** 40 minutes

THE SAND BAR

71 BROADWAY, LEIGH-ON-SEA SS9 1PE TEL: 01702 480067

MON-WED: *10am-12midnight*; THU-SAT: *10am-1am*; SUN: *10am-6pm*

CAPPUCCINO CAFE AND BAKERY

44-46 BROADWAY, LEIGH-ON-SEA SS9 1AH / TEL: 01702 474307

MON-SAT: 8am-5pm; SUN: 9am-4pm

ATELIER GALLERY

96 BROADWAY, LEIGH-ON-SEA SS9 1AB / TEL: 07768 384030

SAT: *10.30am-5.30pm and by appointment*

MYDDELTON HOUSE GARDENS

DESPITE BEING MERE MINUTES from the chicken shops and bookmakers of Enfield, these lovely gardens feel a world away from the city. Though relatively compact, there's plenty to see: early-flowering varieties of crocus are a feature of the Alpine meadow; there's a small Victorian greenhouse; yews line the New River at the edge of the garden. A small (very small — it's a single

room) museum gives some history of the property, and also provides shelter to a pair of lead ostrich sculptures. You may not want to leave such a pretty spot, in which case coffee and cake at the café is recommended.

BULLS CROSS, ENFIELD EN2 9HG / TEL: 03000 030610
DAILY: *10am-4pm (GARDEN 10am-5pm, or dusk if earlier)*
LIVERPOOL STREET TO TURKEY STREET, *approx 20 minute walk* / **JOURNEY TIME** 50 minutes

NORSEY WOOD

BIGGER IS NOT ALWAYS BETTER. In the case of this area of ancient woodland, a fairly compact 165 acres provides habitat for a rich variety of flora and fauna. Designated a Scheduled Ancient Monument and a Site of Special Scientific Interest, along with its natural charms — including ponds, butterflies, bats, dormice and snakes — it's also the unexpected location of two World War One practice trenches.

BILLERICAY, ESSEX CM11 1HA. Entrances in Break Egg Hill, Norsey Close, Deerbank and Norsey Road
TEL: 01277 624553
LIVERPOOL STREET TO BILLERICAY, *approx 15 minute walk* / **JOURNEY TIME** 45 minutes

RICHMOND PARK / PETERSHAM NURSERIES

ALTHOUGH STILL VERY MUCH IN OYSTER CARD TERRITORY, and despite having a wall around its perimeter, Richmond Park has the feel of open country. There are woods, fields, lakes, herds of deer and numerous smaller mammals and insects. Vantage points provide wonderful views over the city, but perhaps still nicer is the aspect looking south towards the North Downs from near Pembroke Lodge Gardens.

Complete the excursion with a visit to Petersham Nurseries. Their Teahouse Café sells simple, delicious and affordable food in a charming greenhouse; or at The Café, a slight misnomer for a place so refined.

RICHMOND PARK
SUMMER, DAILY: *7am-dusk*. WINTER, DAILY: *7.30am-dusk* / TEL: 03000 612200
PETERSHAM NURSERIES
CHURCH LANE, OFF PETERSHAM ROAD, RICHMOND, SURREY TW10 7AB / TEL: 020 8940 5230
MON-SAT: *9am-5pm*; SUN: *11am-5pm*
WATERLOO TO RICHMOND, *approx 20 minute walk* / **JOURNEY TIME** 45 minutes

RUISLIP LIDO & RAILWAY

SANDY BEACHES, A LARGE MANMADE LAKE, narrow gauge trains (including a steamer on some weekends) and ancient woodland add up to a surprisingly grand day out in landlocked Middlesex. When the sun's shining and schools are out it can get unbearably crowded, in which case the woods are a glorious escape. For refreshment there are various kiosks and restaurants, but a picnic may be the best option.

Ruislip tube station is on the Uxbridge branch of both the Metropolitan and Piccadilly lines. H13 and the 331 bus routes stop close by the lido and woods.

RESERVOIR ROAD, RUISLIP HA4 7TY / TEL: 01895 622595
Call for details
BAKER STREET UNDERGROUND TO RUISLIP (METROPOLITAN LINE), *approx 10 minute bus ride* / **JOURNEY TIME** 50 minutes

SOUTHEND-ON-SEA

THE LONGEST PLEASURE PIER in the world is worth travelling for. It's so long — jutting 1.34 miles into the Thames Estuary — that there's a passenger railway. At the pier's far end is The Royal Pavilion, a startling modern structure, built in 2012, that hosts concerts and exhibitions; the café is most welcome on blustery days. It would be a shame to come here and miss out on Adventure Island, a raucous collection of rides with no central admission fee. As counterpoint to the pier, the Cliff Lift is the UK's shortest funicular railway, ascending from the Western Esplanade to the Clifftown conservation area. Those with a yen for something more sophisticated than chips might visit **LA PETITE PETANQUE**, a tea room in a 1930s pavilion with terrace and bowling green.

....

FENCHURCH STREET TO SOUTHEND CENTRAL / **JOURNEY TIME** 51 minutes
LA PETITE PETANQUE
BOWLING GREEN PAVILION, CAMBRIDGE SQUARE GARDENS, SOUTHEND-ON-SEA,
ESSEX SS1 2EZ / TEL: 01702 353208
MON-SAT: *8.30am–7pm;* SUN: *9.30am-7pm*

STRAWBERRY HILL

AN OVER-THE-TOP FANTASY designed as a Thames-side retreat by flamboyant man about Georgian London, Horace Walpole. Work started on the house in the 1740s, making it among the first buildings that can be described as Gothic Revival, yet it's fun rather than forbidding, almost camp in its excess of medieval flourishes, often with plaster and papier mache standing in for carved stone. In Walpole's time the house was filled with his collections, long since scattered, but there's still a lot to see and the extensive grounds are being restored with the same care as has been lavished on the house.

....

268 WALDEGRAVE ROAD, TWICKENHAM TW1 4ST / TEL: 020 8744 1241
MON-WED: *1.30pm-4pm;* SAT-SUN: *12noon-4pm*
WATERLOO TO STRAWBERRY HILL / **JOURNEY TIME** 35 minutes

60-90 MINUTES

BRIGHTON AND HOVE

BROADSTAIRS

COMBINED MILITARY SERVICES MUSEUM

EAST ANGLIAN RAILWAY MUSEUM

FAVERSHAM

HARWICH

HENLEY-ON-THAMES

HEVER CASTLE

LEEDS CASTLE

LEWES

LOSELEY PARK

NATURAL HISTORY MUSEUM AT TRING

OXFORD

PAINSHILL PARK

RAMSGATE

SAFFRON WALDEN

ST LEONARDS-ON-SEA

WHITSTABLE

BRIGHTON AND HOVE

Royal Pavilion

THE PATH FROM LONDON TO BRIGHTON *is so well worn it can sometimes seem that our seaside neighbour has grown too familiar. But tourist money, and the city's substantial population, ensure that new arrivals sprout rapidly alongside old favourites.*

VICTORIA TO BRIGHTON / **JOURNEY TIME** 60 minutes

THINGS TO SEE AND DO

BOOTH MUSEUM OF NATURAL HISTORY

Edward Thomas Booth is another in the long list of eccentric Englishmen about whom it is more fun to read than it would have been to meet. A keen naturalist, he bagged thousands of creatures across the British Isles. He even raised gannets in his garden so that he could shoot them at their physical peak. No surprise then that his museum comprises mainly avian taxidermy and dioramas, some of which is alarmingly red in tooth and claw, along with skeletons — human, animal, bird and even a merman.

194 DYKE ROAD, BRIGHTON BN1 5AA
MON-WED, FRI-SAT: *10am-5pm*
(closed 12noon-1.15pm); SUN: *2pm-5pm*

BRIGHTON MUSEUM AND ART GALLERY

An excellent rainy day option and a beautiful building in its own right (part of the Royal Pavilion complex), the museum offers regular exhibitions alongside a range of small, well-curated permanent displays, including materials relating to Brighton's decadent history. The compact 20th century Art and Design collection features Dali's Mae West Lips Sofa and the upstairs café is a fine place to while away an hour or two over crumpets and tea.

ROYAL PAVILION GARDENS, BRIGHTON BN1 1EE
TUE-SUN: *10am-5pm*

DUKE OF YORK'S PICTUREHOUSE

Arguably Britain's oldest cinema, The Duke is a perfectly intact single-screen picture house and a lovely place to watch a film over a Dark Star beer and a cake from Sticky Fingers. Programming runs to standard arthouse fare, plus the odd classic midnight matinee and kid-friendly weekend morning shows. The sister joint in the North Laine (Dukes at Komedia) is small but well-designed.

PRESTON ROAD, BRIGHTON BN1 4NA /
TEL: 08719 025728

Duke Of York's Picturehouse

OVINGDEAN BEACH

The Undercliff Walk connects Brighton Marina to pretty seaside village Rottingdean — home to Rudyard Kipling, until author-spotting charabanc tours drove him deeper into Sussex. Halfway along the walk (or cycle) lies the beach that locals favour when the town beaches get too rammed with Londoners. It boasts a friendly tea room and winkle-picking/rock-pooling at low tide.

ROYAL PAVILION

Brighton was a sleepy village until George, Prince of Wales, built his stately pleasure dome here to enjoy the sea air and the attentions of his secret bride. And so Brighton was founded on a marriage of the worthy and the illicit, a tradition it continues to this day. The ornate opulence makes the Pavilion an unmissable visit.

4/5 PAVILION BUILDINGS, BRIGHTON BN1 1EE
OCTOBER TO MARCH, DAILY: *10am–5.15pm (last tickets at 4.30pm)*
APRIL TO SEPTEMBER, DAILY: *9.30am–5.45pm (last tickets at 5pm)*

Royal Pavilion

ST ANN'S WELL GARDENS

The prettiest park in town and a genuine alternative to the beach on sunny days, St. Ann's Well is Hampstead Heath in miniature — featuring myriad leafy nooks and crannies and a cracking park café. It occupies the site of a Victorian pleasure garden, where entertainments ran to a monkey house, a hermit in a cave and a film studio credited as the birthplace of editing.

ENTRANCES FROM SOMERHILL ROAD, NIZELLS AVENUE AND FURZE HILL, BRIGHTON BN3

VOLK'S ELECTRIC RAILWAY

Built 1883, Volk's is the oldest operating electric railway in the world and a charming way to complete a seaside perambulation while resting tired legs. The little train toddles along at a civilised pace from the Palace Pier (renamed Brighton Pier, but don't be fooled) via the nudist beach and volleyball courts of Halfway Station to Black Rock, Kemptown's beach. The terminus is a short hop from the mostly charmless Marina. Dedicated promenaders can eschew the yachts and chain restaurants and head straight to the Undercliff Walk towards Ovingdean. NB: The Marina does host a good car boot sale every Sunday morning. Dress warm.

285 MADEIRA DRIVE, BRIGHTON BN2 1EN / TEL: 01273 292718
SEASONAL OPENING, call for details

SHOPS

Magazine

AMSTERDAMMERS

Promising "cycling in elegance and comfort" through a range of imported classic Dutch bikes, new and second-hand. Buy or rent (at reasonable rates) a quality, well designed roadster for a taste of that genteel lowlands two-wheeled vibe. Brighton is rather more hilly than the Netherlands, so you may choose to freewheel down to the sea and along the coast.

UNIT 8, UNDER THE STATION, OFF
TRAFALGAR STREET, BRIGHTON BN1 4FQ /
TEL: 01273 571555
MON-FRI: *9am-6pm*; SAT: *9.30am-5pm*;
SUN: *10am-4pm*

MAGAZINE

Offering exactly what it says on the sign outside, Magazine will give you hope for the future of the printed word. Offering a dazzling array of magazines from across the world, it is well set up for browsing — linger long in the food section, with a fine choice of American and domestic periodicals. Fashion, food, art, design, travel, surfing — all good things are here.

22 TRAFALGAR STREET, BRIGHTON BN1 4EQ /
TEL: 01273 687968
TUE-FRI: *11am-5pm*; SAT: *10am-6pm*;
SUN: *12noon-4pm*

SNOOPER'S PARADISE

If you can't find something you want and don't need in this dusty warren of vintage bits and bobs you simply aren't trying. Short on space, long on variety, each stall reflects a different angle on collectable old stuff — and there are almost always diamonds in the mine for those prepared to dig. Record raccoons with more patience than cash should particularly enjoy the voluminous £3 LP section.

7-8 KENSINGTON GARDENS, BRIGHTON
BN1 4AL / TEL: 01273 602558
MON-SAT: *10am-6pm*; SUN: *11am-4pm*

UTILITY

Occupying an attractive detached building in the North Laine, this shop sells functional goods for the home. The home of the 1950s, that is. These are the sort of useful household items that have slowly disappeared from everyday use, but are still manufactured and still inexpensive. There are brushes for cleaning shoes, dishes, vegetables and scrubbing floors; useful tins; Brown Betty teapots in three sizes, and tea strainers too; carpet beaters; enamelware; tap swirls and spout doileys; they even have carbolic soap.

28A NORTH ROAD, BRIGHTON
BN1 1YB / TEL: 01273 626222
MON-SAT: *10am-6pm*

WORKSHOP LIVING

Brighton now seems almost entirely populated by émigrés from London, to whom the outrageous property prices seem reasonable. Many of the once dilapidated properties have been done up to within an inch of their lives — hence the presence of so many little homeware stores around the North Laine. Workshop purveys well-crafted things with a bleached Scandi-minimalism vibe, suitable for seaside chic.

13A PRINCE ALBERT STREET, BRIGHTON
BN1 1HE / TEL: 01273 731340
MON-SAT: *10am-6pm*; SUN: *12noon-5pm*

Utility

PLACES TO EAT AND DRINK

Bincho Yakitori

BINCHO YAKITORI

Bincho (and Goemon Ramen down the street) may herald a revival for dowdy Preston Street. A top-shelf exemplar of the Japanese art of the grill. Informal, inn-style dishes, heavy on seafood and meat skewers, but with vegan options (it is Brighton, after all).

63 PRESTON STREET, BRIGHTON BN1 2HE / TEL: 01273 779021

TUE-THU: *6pm-10pm;* FRI-SAT: *5.30pm-10.30pm;* SUN: *5.30pm-10pm*

BRIGHTON SMOKEHOUSE

Under the arches between the piers, the Smokehouse is a genuine Brighton institution and the best value lunch on the front. Jack and Linda Mills smoke locally sourced fish over oak and applewood and serve it hot and simple in sandwiches to take away. Ideal for a picnic on the stones.

201 KING'S ROAD ARCHES, BRIGHTON BN1 1NB / TEL: 07578 079501

DAILY: *9am-5pm*

The Flour Pot

CURRY LEAF CAFÉ

A tremendously (and deservedly) successful modern Indian café . During the day, the emphasis is on affordable lunch fare — thali platters, naan wraps and delicious dosas. Evenings offer sophisticated curries, matched with an exceptional range of beers. Must try: mango and cardamom ice cream, from local gelateria Boho Gelato.

60 SHIP STREET, BRIGHTON BN1 1AE /
TEL: 01273 207070

SUN-THU: *12noon-3pm & 5.30pm-9.30pm*;
FRI-SAT: *12noon-3pm & 6pm-10.30pm*

THE FLOUR POT

It's all about the bread. The Flour Pot sells arguably the best in the South (with a nod to Flint Owl of Lewes and Sugardough of Hove) and the quality ingredients and attention to detail announce themselves from the first bite of their intensely chewy seeded sourdough. Their North Laine flagship serves equally excellent snacks, lunches and coffee with a warm, homey atmosphere.

40 SYDNEY STREET, BRIGHTON BN1 4EP /
TEL: 01273 621942

MON-SAT: *8am-7pm*; SUN: *9am-6pm*

(L) James French Photography (R) Emma Gutteridge

GROUND

Brightonians spend more on coffee per capita than anywhere else in Britain. The centre of town features a range of independents, dominated by the many branches of Small Batch. The more interesting (and customer-friendly) spots are in local neighbourhoods, e.g. Tilt in Fiveways and Ground in bohemian Kemptown, where coffee knowledge is worn lightly, the snacks are delicious and the barista will not delay taking your order to discuss tattoos with colleagues.

34-36 ST GEORGE'S ROAD, BRIGHTON
BN2 1ED / TEL: 01273 696441
MON-FRI: *7am-5pm*; SAT-SUN: *8am-5pm*

THE HEART AND HAND

Brighton, per Keith Waterhouse, has the air of a town that is perpetually helping the police with their inquiries. Hang around in a proper North Laine boozer for a sense of what he was getting at. There may be better pubs in town (we suggest The Great Eastern for whisky and The Evening Star for beer) but none can touch the Heart for a proper bohemian vibe and what is undoubtedly the greatest jukebox in town, best enjoyed over a pint of Harveys' Sussex Best.

75 NORTH ROAD, BRIGHTON
BN1 1YD / TEL: 01273 683320
DAILY: *12noon-12midnight*

KOR-PAN

The Open Market is an attempted reinvention of Brighton's traditional fruit and veg marketplace. It hosts a smattering of interesting stalls, including a great used bookshop and a collection of fantastic cheap eats: come here for falafel, Greek and Bangladeshi (the latter from Mohammed Spice of Life). Kor-Pan is the most exciting new addition — a fusion of Korean and Japanese cuisines, with the former exemplified in an intensely spicy, greasy, moreish kimchee pancake.

THE OPEN MARKET, MARSHALLS ROW,
BRIGHTON BN1 4JU

Curry Leaf Cafe

Sunbirds Deli

MAROCCO'S

This Italian restaurant is the reason Brightonians turn right when they reach the seafront; their home-made gelato has been enlivening promenade strolls since 1969. On sunny days the queue stretches round the block and hungry children stare balefully at your melting stracciatella.

8 KINGS ESPLANADE, BRIGHTON BN3 2WA / TEL: 01273 203764

MON-THU: *8am-10pm;*
FRI-SAT: *8am-10.30pm;* SUN: *8am-9.30pm*

PIZZA 500

In the shadow of the railway viaduct and to the soundtrack of rumbling trains, Pizza 500 features Italian pizza made by actual Italians who know that the quality of the crust comes before the novelty of the toppings. There's a selection of home-made gelato too.

83 PRESTON ROAD, BRIGHTON BN1 4QG / TEL: 01273 911933

TUE-SAT: *6pm-11pm;* SUN: *6pm-10pm*

SILO

Innovative restaurant, not shy in proclaiming its sustainable ethos. If you don't mind drinking from a jam jar, you'll enjoy the bright, industrial space and a menu heavy on the local and seasonal in creative combinations, with food that's as tasty as it is ethical.

39 UPPER GARDNER STREET, BRIGHTON BN1 4AN / TEL: 01273 674259

MON: *8.30am-5pm;* TUE-SAT: *8.30am-11pm;*
SUN: *10am-5pm*

SUNBIRDS DELI

A ray of light from a hole in the wall on the otherwise unlovely London Road, Sunbirds offers culinary adventurers delightful (Kurdish) meze platters and exotic desserts, including many that are gluten-free and vegan, and no less delicious for that.

108 LONDON ROAD, BRIGHTON BN1 4JG / TEL: 07427 695119

MON-FRI: *8am-6.30pm;* SAT: *9am-7pm*

Wolfies of Hove

Silo

UNITHAI ORIENTAL MARKET

At the back of an Asian mini-mart in Hove is a genuine secret. A few tables and chairs (at least one of which you may have to share), a short menu, slow and sometimes begrudging service and the most authentically delicious Thai food this side of London.

10 CHURCH ROAD, HOVE BN3 2FL /
TEL: 01273 733246

MON-THU: *11.30am-3:30pm;*
FRI: *11.30am-8.30pm;* SAT: *11.30am-8.30pm*

WOLFIES OF HOVE

The best fish and chips in Brighton is now in Hove, or as it has traditionally differentiated itself from its tackier neighbour. Wolfies do proper fish and chips, pies and mushy peas, unusual specials (spicy squid) with gluten-free options. Cash only.

90 GOLDSTONE VILLAS, HOVE BN3 3RU /
TEL: 01273 962395

MON-FRI: *12noon-3pm & 4.30pm-10pm;*
SAT: *12noon-10pm;* SUN: *2pm-10pm*

BROADSTAIRS

SANDWICHED BETWEEN MARGATE AND RAMSGATE, Broadstairs is smaller and quainter than its neighbours and a destination in itself. Charles Dickens spent his summers here, inadvertently launching a heritage industry the end result of which is the "Charles Dickens Gourmet Hand-Made Cheeseburger". (It really exists, we won't say where.)

A gelato at **MORELLI'S** is obligatory, as it has been since the 1930s. Though the family now have franchises in Manila, Kuwait and Dallas, the original branch has the classic look and feel of the British seaside.

WYATT & JONES represents the current seaside revival, a Modern British restaurant from its "torched mackerel, radish & kale 'seaweed', brown bread puree" to the austere interior with lovely sea views. Of many pubs, **THE THIRTY-NINE STEPS** is notable for excellent ale and paying homage to a literary figure other than Charles Dickens — John Buchan wrote The 39 Steps while convalescing in Broadstairs. The remnants of the cliff steps that inspired him are still just visible at nearby North Foreland. From Viking Bay it's just a half hour beach walk to Ramsgate in the west, but be sure to check tides.

Tip: Folk Week, in early August, can strain this little town to breaking point.

Wyatt & Jones

....

ST PANCRAS INTERNATIONAL TO BROADSTAIRS **JOURNEY TIME** 80 MINUTES

MORELLI'S

14 VICTORIA PARADE, BROADSTAIRS CT10 1QS / TEL: 01843 862500

MON-FRI: *8am-5pm;* SAT-SUN: *8am-7pm*

WYATT & JONES

23-27 HARBOUR STREET, BROADSTAIRS CT10 1EU / TEL: 01843 865126

Seasonal opening, call for details

THE THIRTY-NINE STEPS

5 CHARLOTTE STREET, BROADSTAIRS CT10 1LR

DAILY: *12noon-11pm*

COMBINED MILITARY SERVICES MUSEUM

AT SOME POINT ON THE JOURNEY HERE, you'll be convinced you've taken a wrong turn. Press on, past Tesco and Kwik Fit, into a dreary industrial estate at which point a missile sitting in a car park is sufficient clue that you've made it. Inside are vast quantities of weapons, uniforms from all British armed services going back to the 17th century, and a considerable archive of equipment from Special Forces. The showstopper is the collection of rare, often unique and frequently bizarre, devices used by husband and wife spies Peter and Prue Mason during World War Two.

STATION ROAD, MALDON, ESSEX CM9 4LQ / TEL: 01621 841826
WED-SUN (AND BANK HOLIDAYS): *10.30am-5pm*
LIVERPOOL STREET TO CHELMSFORD, *35 minute bus ride or approx 15 minute walk*
JOURNEY TIME 85 minutes

EAST ANGLIAN RAILWAY MUSEUM

BEING HOUSED IN A WORKING RAILWAY STATION certainly lends authenticity to this museum. It also means that every half hour the careful illusion of the age of steam is shattered when a modern train pulls in. The site includes signal boxes, a new restoration shed and, of course, a great many standard gauge and miniature trains, which on event days are eased into stately action. Surrounded by beautiful countryside, and with plenty of indoor space, the EARM has year-round appeal. Visit their site for events that range from a Day Out With Thomas the Tank Engine to beer festivals in the goods shed.

CHAPPEL AND WAKES COLNE STATION, WAKES COLNE, ESSEX CO6 2DS /
TEL: 01206 242524
DAILY: *10am-4.30pm, dusk if earlier*
LIVERPOOL STREET TO CHAPPEL AND WAKES COLNE *(change at Marks Tey)* /
JOURNEY TIME 65 minutes

FAVERSHAM

A TOWN SO PRETTY it will have you peering into estate agents' windows within minutes of arrival. In truth there's no single destination that makes it worth visiting, rather a combination of things. Wonderful, varied architecture, including many timber-framed medieval buildings, most visible in Abbey Street. Charity shops, junk shops and antique shops are very well represented, dotted around the centre of town with another clump in **STANDARD QUAY**, down by the creek where boats are still repaired. This is also hometown of Shepherd Neame, Britain's oldest brewer, whose pretty pubs are particularly well maintained here, best being **THE BEAR INN**, with its polar bear painting in the public bar and a cosy snug, and there are two-hour tours of the brewery too, including a 30-minute tasting. As an alternative, **THE PHOENIX TAVERN** has a wider range of beer, shareable food and two open fires — there;s a garden too, though less charming. Market days are the best time to visit, and there are a lot of them, all held in the medieval Market Place — Tuesday, Friday and Saturday and on the first Sunday of every month there's a vintage and antiques market.

. . . .

ST PANCRAS INTERNATIONAL
TO FAVERSHAM /
JOURNEY TIME 65 MINUTES
STANDARD QUAY, FAVERSHAM ME13 7BS
DAILY: *10am-4pm*

UPSTAIRS DOWNSTAIRS
88-90 WEST STREET, FAVERSHAM
ME13 7JQ / TEL: 01795 227190
DAILY: *10am-5pm*

THE BEAR INN
MARKET PLACE, FAVERSHAM ME13 7AG
/ TEL: 01795 532668
MON-SAT: *10.30am-11pm;*
SUN: *11.30am-11pm*

THE PHOENIX INN
98-99 ABBEY STREET, FAVERSHAM
ME13 7BH / TEL: 01795 591462
DAILY: *12noon-11.45pm*

HARWICH

WHEN LOOKING AT THE SEA seems like a better idea than wading in it, this historic little town at the north-eastern tip of Essex may be a good option. There's plenty to see, including the **REDOUBT FORT**, a circular Napoleonic-era fortress, several museums devoted to aspects of the town's maritime history, the tiny **HALFPENNY PIER** jutting into the sea and **LIGHT VESSEL LV18**, a former floating lighthouse, that's now a memorial to Pirate Radio. If the weather turns, the **ELECTRIC PALACE** is one of the oldest purpose-built cinemas in the UK, complete with glorious exterior, and there are several pubs to warm up, among them **THE NEW BELL** and **THE ALMA INN**.

....

LIVERPOOL STREET TO HARWICH TOWN *(change at Manningtree)* / **JOURNEY TIME** 85 MINUTES
REDOUBT FORT
MAIN ROAD, HARWICH CO12 3LT / TEL: 01255 553610
MAY-AUGUST, DAILY: *10am-4pm;* SEPTEMBER-APRIL: *Sun: 10am-4pm*
LIGHT VESSEL LV18
MARCH-OCTOBER, DAILY: *11am-4pm*
ELECTRIC PALACE CINEMA
KING'S QUAY STREET, HARWICH CO12 3ER / TEL: 01255 553333
THE NEW BELL INN
OUTPART EASTWARD, HARWICH CO12 3EN / TEL: 01255 503545
MON-SAT: *11am-12midnight;* SUN: *12noon-12midnight*
THE ALMA INN
25 KING'S HEAD STREET, HARWICH CO12 3EE / TEL: 01255 318681
SUN-THU: *12noon-11pm;* FRI-SAT: *12noon-12midnight*

River And Rowing Museum

HENLEY-ON-THAMES

IN KENNETH GRAHAME'S THE WIND IN THE WILLOWS, Ratty, Mole, Toad and Badger all make their home close to Henley. Those characters have been brought vividly back to life at the **RIVER AND ROWING MUSEUM**, which displays three-dimensional renderings of the original E.H. Shepard illustrations. The river itself is this pretty town's most alluring feature, ideally viewed from a boat (available to hire from several local firms) or, perhaps less precariously, from **THE ANGEL ON THE BRIDGE**, a picturesque pub and the town's only one on the river. Walks into the surrounding countryside or along the Thames path are recommended.

The town's greatest influx of visitors is for the Henley Regatta, held from Wednesday to Sunday over the first weekend in July. All great fun, of course, but the crowds can be a bit much.

....

PADDINGTON TO HENLEY-ON-THAMES *(change at Twyford)*

JOURNEY TIME 65 minutes

RIVER AND ROWING MUSEUM

MILL LANE, HENLEY-ON-THAMES RG9 1BF / TEL: 01491 415600

DAILY: *10am-5pm*

THE ANGEL ON THE BRIDGE

NEXT TO THE BRIDGE, HENLEY-ON-THAMES RG9 1BH / TEL: *01491 410678*

MON-FRI: *12noon-3pm & 6pm-10pm*; SAT: *11.30am-10pm*; SUN: *11.30am-7pm*

HEVER CASTLE

THE PUBLIC'S UNDIMMED FASCINATION with Henry VIII and his unfortunate wives is central to the appeal of Hever, childhood home of Anne Boleyn and later Anne of Cleves. The king and his consorts appear in contemporary portraits and also, lamentably, in the form of actors and mannequins, both of which detract from rather than enhance the experience of the castle. A few elements of the original 13th-century structure remain but it's been significantly altered, notably by William Waldorf Astor, at one time the richest man in America, who acquired the castle in 1903, building a "Tudor village" among other fun but inauthentic additions, and landscaping the grounds to great effect. In fact the gardens alone make a visit worthwhile. Huge and magnificent, among the highlights are chess set topiary, rose garden, boating lake, yew maze and water maze. Allow time to explore a collection of miniature model houses, accessible from the shop.

HEVER, EDENBRIDGE, KENT TN8 7NG / TEL: 01732 865224
APRIL-OCTOBER, DAILY: *10.30am-4.30pm* (CASTLE *12noon-4.30pm*)
NOVEMBER-MARCH: *Seasonal opening hours apply, call for details*
LONDON BRIDGE TO HEVER, *approx 25 minute walk* / **JOURNEY TIME** 65 minutes

LEEDS CASTLE

WITH RARE EXCEPTIONS, castles are ill-served by public transport, a fact not unrelated to prior concerns about impregnability. Leeds is no exception, but the minor slog is worth it; a greater impediment to entry is the £24 charged for admission. But this sum gets you access to magnificent grounds and gardens — including a maze and grotto — and the castle itself, and is valid for 12 months. A castle has stood on this site since the 12th century, but what we see today bears only the vaguest relation to that original, ever more fancifully reimagined throughout the 19th and early 20th centuries, resulting in the fairytale vision we now enjoy. It's over the top, even a little ridiculous in parts, but with blue skies and the sun reflecting in the lake, the old place can still take your breath away.

MAIDSTONE, KENT ME17 1PL / TEL: 01622 765400
APRIL-SEPTEMBER, DAILY: *10am-6pm* (CASTLE *10.30am-4.30pm*)
OCTOBER-MARCH, DAILY: *10am-5pm* (CASTLE *10.30am-3pm*)
VICTORIA TO BEARSTED, *coach shuttle service available* / **JOURNEY TIME** 85 minutes

Southover Grange Gardens

LEWES

YOU WILL BE WELL FED AND WATERED in this pretty town, nestled in a nook of the South Downs. The first branch of the **BILL'S** chain is here (you may even see Bill himself keeping an eye on things). Munching through breakfast, one can see why the formula has been such a success. Close by, **LE MAGASIN** is a rather more tranquil option with a similar atmosphere and excellent food. Situated in an attractive courtyard between two of the town's many antique shops, **THE BUTTERCUP CAFÉ** is a good spot for an early lunch. Bag an outside seat in the sun and make the most of the limited menu of just three or four dishes which run out by 2pm. **THE LEWES ARMS** is a round-fronted corner pub that wears its eccentricity with pride (the World Pea Throwing Championship trophy lives behind the bar), but the lamb burgers with feta cheese are recommended and they serve the local ale, Harveys. Should more refreshment be needed at any

The Lewes Arms

Bill's

Fifteenth Century Bookshop

point, the LANSDOWN ARMS with its indoor tree, THE ELEPHANT AND CASTLE and the more local-feeling GARDENER'S ARMS are all good choices.

LEWES PRIORY was destroyed on the orders of Henry VIII, but the monk's lavatories can still be made out while wandering among the ruins. The rest of the Priory was used to build SOUTHOVER GRANGE, the gardens of which are open to the public and quite magnificent, with impeccable flower beds and mature trees. A hole-in-the-wall tea counter does a fine line in traditional cakes.

There are a number of antique, vintage and bookshops to explore on Cliffe High Street, and it's worth climbing up steep Keere Street to visit the FIFTEENTH CENTURY BOOKSHOP, which is as good as it sounds.

A pleasant, but fairly demanding walk of an hour or two can be had from CHAPEL HILL to the operatic village of GLYNDE — with magnificent views of Lewes, tiptoeing through herds of cattle, skylark spotting, a dewpond, and THE TREVOR ARMS in Glynde for refreshment at the end. Trains to London via Lewes run from Glynde hourly.

....

VICTORIA TO LEWES
JOURNEY TIME 60 minutes
BILL'S
56 CLIFFE HIGH STREET, LEWES BN7 2AN /
TEL: 01273 476918
MON-FRI: *8am-10.30pm;* SAT: *8am-11pm;*
SUN: *9am-10.30pm*
LE MAGASIN
50A CLIFFE HIGH STREET, LEWES BN7 2AN /
TEL: 01273 474720
MON-WED: *8am–5pm;* THU-SAT: *8am-9pm;*
SUN: *9am-4pm*
THE BUTTERCUP CAFÉ
15 MALLING STREET, LEWES BN7 2RA /
TEL: 01273 477664
MON-SAT: *9.30am-4pm*
THE LEWES ARMS
MOUNT PLACE, LEWES BN7 1YH /
TEL: 01273 473152
MON-THU: *11am-11pm;* FRI-SAT: *11am-
12midnight;* SUN: *12noon-11pm*
LANSDOWN ARMS
36 LANSDOWN PLACE, LEWES BN7 2JU /
TEL: 01273 470711

SUN-THU: *12noon-11pm;*
FRI-SAT: *12noon-12midnight*
THE ELEPHANT AND CASTLE
WHITE HILL, LEWES BN7 2DJ /
TEL: 01273 473797
MON-THU: *11.30am-11pm;* FRI-SAT: *11.30am-
12midnight;* SUN: *12noon-11p*m
GARDENER'S ARMS
46 CLIFFE HIGH STREET, LEWES BN7 2AN /
TEL: 01273 474808
MON-SAT: *11am-11pm;* SUN: *12noon-10.30pm*
LEWES PRIORY
COCKSHUT ROAD, LEWES BN7 1HP
SOUTHOVER GRANGE GARDENS
SOUTHOVER ROAD, LEWES BN7 1TP
DAILY: *8.30am-dusk*
FIFTEENTH CENTURY BOOKSHOP
99-100 HIGH STREET, LEWES BN7 1XH /
TEL: 01273 474160
MON-SAT: *10am-5.30pm*
THE TREVOR ARMS
THE STREET, GLYNDE BN8 6SS /
TEL: 01273 858208
DAILY: *11.30am-11pm*

LOSELEY PARK

THERE ARE EASIER PLACES TO REACH by public transport, but if the sun's out the walk of around a mile through lovely parkland is no great hardship. After upgrading their old digs to this grand manor house ahead of a visit by Elizabeth I, the More-Molyneux family stayed put. As you probably would too if this was home. Weddings and events keep the wolf from the door, and in summer months the house and gardens are open to the public.

Filled with original art and furnishings, it features a fireplace hewn from a single colossal piece of chalk, magnificent carved wood panelling, a minstrel's gallery and a fine collection of royal and family portraits — including one of Anne Boleyn. The walled garden, based on a design by Gertrude Jekyll, is divided into a sequence of rooms: formal Rose Garden, the more rambling Flower Garden, Vegetable Garden and a large Herb Garden.

Loseley's famous ice cream, though no longer made on site, is still available in the tea room along with other refreshments.

GUILDFORD, SURREY GU3 1HS / TEL: 01483 304440
SUMMER: SUN-THU: *11am-5pm* (HOUSE *by tour only*)
WATERLOO TO GUILDFORD, *10 minute bus ride or approx 20 minute walk* /
JOURNEY TIME 70 minutes

NATURAL HISTORY MUSEUM AT TRING

FOUR THOUSAND SPECIMENS displayed in floor-to-ceiling, glass-fronted wood and iron cases, just as they were when the museum opened in 1892 to house the collection of Walter Rothschild, zebra-riding scion of the banking dynasty. This remarkable collection includes birds, insects and mammals large and small, from miniature lapdogs to the extinct great auk. Tring station is two miles from the Museum which can be reached by bus or taxi.

....

THE WALTER ROTHSCHILD BUILDING, AKEMAN STREET, TRING, HERTFORDSHIRE HP23 6AP / TEL: 020 7942 6171

MON-SAT: *10am-5pm*; SUN: *2pm-5pm*

EUSTON TO TRING, *15 minute bus ride or approx 45 minute walk* / **JOURNEY TIME** 60 minutes

Pitt Rivers Museum

A DEGREE OF PLANNING IS KEY *to getting the most from this busy and congested city. The highlights are significant but it's spread out and progress can be slow. Should hunger strike, beware that chain shops and restaurants have a powerful hold. Time spent roaming the colleges is never wasted, and if the weather is fine, a trip to the river is essential.*

. . . .

PADDINGTON TO OXFORD / **JOURNEY TIME** 60 MINUTES

THINGS TO SEE AND DO

ASHMOLEAN MUSEUM

A major renovation in 2009 brought light and space to what had long been a fusty place, and with it came a satisfying rethink of how objects are displayed. There's an emphasis here on finding similarities across different cultures that highlights trade and the exchange of ideas as well as universal, human qualities that persist across time. This is a world class museum with a collection that's stuffed with relics from the ancient world, fine art from the medieval period to the present, textiles and a variety of curiosities including Guy Fawkes' lantern. Temporary exhibitions and talks are an additional draw.

BEAUMONT STREET, OXFORD OX1 2PH / TEL: 01865 278000

TUE-SUN & BANK HOLIDAY MON: *10am–5pm*

Modern Art Oxford

CHRIST CHURCH GALLERY

Here you'll find remarkable works by Leonardo, Michelangelo, Raphael, Dürer and Rubens. The purpose-built gallery, an elegant structure from 1968, is worth seeing in itself.

CHRIST CHURCH, ST ALDATES, OXFORD OX1 1DP / TEL: 01865 276172

OCTOBER-MAY, MON, WED-SAT: *10.30am-1pm & 2pm-4.30pm;* SUN: *2pm-4.30pm*
JUNE, MON, WED-SAT: *10.30am-5pm;* Sun: *2pm-5pm*
JULY-SEPTEMBER, MON-SAT: *10.30am-5pm;* SUN: *2pm-5pm*

MODERN ART OXFORD

In contrast to the heritage-heavy feel of most of the town, this gallery is focussed on contemporary art, frequently at its most uncompromising. There's no permanent collection, so check their website for details of exhibitions. Even if nothing on show appeals, the gallery's café is a pleasant space to spend time, and excellent value too.

30 PEMBROKE STREET, OXFORD OX1 1BP / TEL: 01865 722733

TUE-SAT: *11am-6pm;* SUN: *12noon-5pm*

PITT RIVERS MUSEUM

Located at the end of the University's Museum of Natural History, the Pitt Rivers is as strange as it is wonderful. Wood and glass cases are packed with exhibits of varying provenance and antiquity — musical instruments, masks, toys, weapons, coins. Drawers beneath the cases, some of which can be opened by visitors, contain still more objects. The room is dark, totem poles loom; canoes, spears, paddles are suspended from the ceilings. The collection rambles over three floors, delivering a different perspective on the idiosyncrasies and similarities of all humankind.

SOUTH PARKS ROAD, OXFORD OX1 3PW /
TEL: 01865 270927
MON: *12noon-4.30pm;*
TUE-SUN: *10am-4.30pm*

UNIVERSITY OF OXFORD BOTANIC GARDEN

Small but splendid, and soon to celebrate its 400th anniversary. Situated in the city centre, on the banks of the Cherwell, between Merton and Magdalen colleges, glimpses of which loom into view above abundant flora. Seven glasshouses showcase plants from around the world, guaranteeing that there's always something to see regardless of the season. The walled garden houses scientific collections, including woodland and medicinal plants, and the lower garden has ornamental plantings. No café but picnics are welcome.

ROSE LANE, OXFORD OX1 4AZ /
TEL: 01865 286690
SEASONAL OPENING, call for details

SHOPS

BLACKWELL'S BOOKSHOP

More than just a flagship for a national chain, this vast bookshop is one of the best in the land. Given its location, academic titles are well represented, but the travel, fiction and children's sections are also excellent. Opened in 1879, as a seller of rare and second-hand books, that side of the business continues here. Across the road, is their specialist Art and Poster Shop.

48-51 BROAD STREET, OX1 3BQ /
TEL: 01865 792792
MON: *9am-6.30pm;* TUE: *9.30am-6.30pm;*
WED-SAT: *9am-6.30pm;* SUN: *11am-5pm*

OBJECTS OF USE

An appealing store selling a variety of functional and attractive tools and items for the home that are as pleasing to look at as they are to use: a reindeer leather coin purse; Japanese knives and axes; German nutcrackers; Finnish thermos flasks; Welsh blankets. Their range of wooden toys is noteworthy and quite sophisticated enough to make as good a gift for a grown-up as they would a child.

6 LINCOLN HOUSE, MARKET STREET,
OXFORD OX1 3EQ / TEL: 01865 241705
MON-SAT: *10am-5pm;* SUN: *11am-4pm*

Objects Of Use

OXFORD COVERED MARKET

The chain restaurants that have such a firm grip on this city are happily absent from this market, where you can find a place to sit down and eat or just pick up something for later. In the latter camp, pies from **DAVID JOHN** are eminently portable and **NECTAR**'s cold-pressed juices may be just the burst of energy a weary traveller needs to keep going. For those wanting to take a load off, there are many options among which cheerful greasy spoon **BROWN'S CAFÉ** is a favourite.

MARKET STREET, OXFORD OX1 3DZ
MON-SAT: *8am-5.30pm;* SUN: *10am-4pm*

SANDERS OF OXFORD

Housed in a 16th-century building are many thousands of books, maps and prints as varied in subject as they are in price, encompassing Victorian caricatures, 18th-century celestial charts and contemporary prints. So abundant and engrossing is their stock, it's tempting to think of this as a gallery rather than a shop, but everything is for sale and while some prices are daunting, charming prints can be had for quite reasonable sums.

SALUTATION HOUSE, 104 HIGH STREET, OXFORD, OX1 4BW / TEL: 01865 242590
MON-SAT: *10am-6pm;* SUN: *11am-5pm*

The Anchor

PLACES TO EAT AND DRINK

THE ANCHOR

A large slightly municipal-looking 1930s pub, stripped back and renovated in modish, austere style. There are no cosy sofas and foaming tankards here, food is the thing — modern, mostly British and very tasty. We suggest the 16 ounce Chateaubriand for two. Vegetarians are well catered for, with not a sweet potato tart in sight. A postprandial amble in Port Meadow, directly across from here, should be just the ticket.

2 HAYFIELD ROAD, OXFORD OX2 6TT /
TEL: 018655 10282
MON-FRI: *9am-11pm;* SAT-SUN: *10am-11pm*

THE BEAR INN

As traditional as The Anchor is modern, Oxford's oldest pub (it's been here at least 500 years, some claim longer) is cosy, wood-panelled and covered in severed ties from punters past. It's a good place to plan the rest of your day, or wind down after exploring. Sausages, burgers, fish and chips and pies are hearty and much as you'd expect; mushrooms on toast is simple and sustaining.

6 ALFRED STREET, OXFORD OX1 4EH /
TEL: 01865 728164
MON-THU: *11am-11pm;* FRI-SAT: *11am-12midnight;* SUN: *11.30am-10.30pm*

PAINSHILL PARK

CONSTRUCTED IN THE 18TH CENTURY and considerably restored in recent years, this 158-acre garden is a peaceful, romantic spot. Enhancing its appeal are the follies that dot the landscape, among them a ruined abbey, hermitage, gothic tower, Turkish tent and a unique crystal grotto (for which opening times are limited), all artfully positioned for the benefit of visitors.

PORTSMOUTH ROAD, COBHAM, SURREY KT11 1JE / TEL: 01932 868113
MARCH-OCTOBER, DAILY: *10am-4.30pm, dusk if earlier*
NOVEMBER-FEBRUARY, DAILY: *10am-3pm, dusk if earlier*
WATERLOO TO COBHAM & STOKE D'ABERNON, *10 minute bus, 5 minute walk* /
JOURNEY TIME 60 minutes

RAMSGATE

Madeira Gardens

RAMSGATE ISN'T A SEASIDE TOWN AS SUCH. *Although it has sandy beaches, its heart is the charming Georgian harbour, making it a good year-round option, less quiet off-season than its Kiss-Me-Quick neighbours Broadstairs and Margate. The 15-20-minute walk from the station into town does little to build enthusiasm, but there are buses to the seafront or, for about £4, a cab will take you there.*

ST PANCRAS INTERNATIONAL TO RAMSGATE / **JOURNEY TIME** 75 MINUTES

THINGS TO SEE AND DO

MADEIRA GARDENS, EAST CLIFF

Engagingly eccentric miniature ornamental gardens, constructed in the early 19th century, like a Victorian slice of Disneyland, with a waterfall, rocks, small trees, and a few benches from which to gaze out to sea.

RAMSGATE TUNNELS

Making use of a disused trainline that deposited holiday-makers directly onto the front, a network of tunnels was constructed for use as air raid shelters during World War Two. Only recently re-opened, the tunnels have become a popular attraction (despite obligatory hard-hats) which means that advance booking is recommended.
MARINA ESPLANADE, RAMSGATE CT11 8LN / TEL: 01843 588123
SEASONAL OPENING

Ramsgate Tunnels

SPENCER SQUARE, VALE SQUARE, LIVERPOOL LAWN, GUILDFORD LAWN

In a town notable for its supply of Georgian and Victorian buildings, the above addresses are particularly striking, a stroll taking them all in is not arduous. Van Gogh spent a few months in Ramsgate in 1876, both the house he stayed in and school at which he taught are in Spencer Square, marked with plaques. The Square now has tennis courts and a little café.

SHOPS

ARCH 16

A few doors along from Archive (see page 66), a pleasingly haphazard collection of items for those with a taste for the hunt: shop signs and old radios, light fixtures and musical instruments, mangey taxidermy and 1950s kitchenware.

ARCH 16, MILITARY ROAD, RAMSGATE CT11 9LG / TEL: 07474 444481
MON-FRI: *12noon-5pm;*
SAT-SUN: *10am-5.30pm*

PARAPHERNALIA

For 20th century furniture, paintings and ephemera, all of it in excellent condition and fairly priced. Vintage Ramsgate postcards make an inexpensive and lightweight souvenir.

2 ADDINGTON STREET, RAMSGATE CT11 9JL / TEL: 07434 979557
SUN, THU-FRI: *11am-5pm;*
SAT: *10am-5pm*

VINYLHEAD

It's a café with a nice little garden — and their ice cream's good too — but it's also a record shop, with a small but diverse stock that throws up some surprises.

2-3 THE BROADWAY, ADDINGTON STREET, RAMSGATE CT11 9JN /
TEL: 07901 334653
DAILY: *9am-5pm*

Arch 16

Paraphernalia

PLACES TO EAT AND DRINK

The Ravensgate Arms

QUEEN CHARLOTTE

The coast's allure to eccentrics is in evidence at this jolly pub, a mainstay of this handsome street, once one of the town's main shopping areas. With a mischievous anti-authoritarian streak, a party atmosphere frequently prevails.

57 ADDINGTON STREET, RAMSGATE CT11 9JJ / TEL: 01843 570703

WED: *5.30pm-10pm;* THU: *5.30pm-11pm;* FRI-SAT: *5.30pm-12midnight;* SUN: *12noon-6pm*

THE RAVENSGATE ARMS

This friendly, unpretentious pub has the best selection of beer in town, selected from across the UK in cask, keg, can and bottle. There's a very satisfying food offering too: burgers (including vegetarian), salads and mac and cheese are all recommended.

56-58 KING STREET, RAMSGATE CT11 8NY / TEL: 01843 582570

DAILY: *12noon-11pm*

ARCHIVE HOMESTORE & KITCHEN

A 2016 arrival that heralds the town's gently shifting demographic. Enjoy coffee, a meal or just browse the selection of books, toys and homewares in this clever reworking of an an old harbour arch, arranged over two floors and filled with natural light.

17 MILITARY ROAD, RAMSGATE CT11 9LG / TEL: 01843 580666

WED-MON: *9.30am-5pm*

FLAVOURS BY KUMAR

In old pub premises on a side street, outward appearances give no hint to the quality of this Indian restaurant, whose chef-proprietor brings rare subtlety to his dishes.

2 EFFINGHAM STREET, RAMSGATE CT11 9AT / TEL: 01843 852631

DAILY: *12noon-2.30pm & 5.30pm-10pm*

PETER'S FISH FACTORY / SUNRISE

Ideally located on the sea front, but locals say Sunrise pips it for quality.

PETER'S, 96 HARBOUR PARADE, RAMSGATE CT11 8LP / TEL: 01843 853272

DAILY: *11am-11pm*

SUNRISE FISH & CHIPS, 22 QUEEN STREET, RAMSGATE CT11 9DR / TEL: 01843 446453

MON-THU: *11am-9pm;* FRI-SAT: *10am-9pm;* SUN: *1pm-8pm*

ROYAL HARBOUR BRASSERIE

At the far end of the harbour wall, it takes a few minutes to walk here. Open all day for meals, snacks and drinks. In summer you may glimpse France from the terrace.

ROYAL HARBOUR PARADE, RAMSGATE CT11 8LS / TEL: 01843 599059

SUMMER, DAILY: *11am-11pm;* WINTER: *Call for details*

Archive

SAFFRON WALDEN

THE ESSEX JOKE IS ELEGANTLY REBUFFED by the mere presence of this beautiful, civilised town, still essentially Medieval in layout and packed with wonderful buildings from the 12th century on. Time seems to have passed Saffron Walden by, perhaps a result of the railway station being closed in 1964, which means a longish walk, taxi ride, or a bus from **AUDLEY END** station — named for the wonderful Jacobean house and gardens, well worth visiting in its own right. **BRIDGE END GARDEN**, laid out in the 1820s, is a series of ornamental gardens, including a yew hedge maze. **THE FRY ART GALLERY** has as its focus 20th century artists associated with the area, among them Edward Bawden, Eric Ravilious and John Aldridge, represented in a collection of paintings, prints and wallpapers. Nourishment can be found at **THE KINGS ARMS**, which benefits from an open fire when it's chilly and outside space when it isn't. **ANGELA REED** is a more refined option for cake, coffee or a light lunch.

. . . .

LIVERPOOL STREET TO AUDLEY END, *approx 5 minute bus ride* /
JOURNEY TIME 60 minutes
ANGELA REED
5-7 MARKET HILL, SAFFRON WALDEN CB10 1HQ / TEL: 01799 520056
MON-SAT: *9am-5pm*
AUDLEY END HOUSE & GARDENS
OFF LONDON ROAD, SAFFRON WALDEN CB11 4JF / TEL: 01799 522842
SEASONAL OPENING, call for details
BRIDGE END GARDEN
ENTRANCES IN CASTLE STREET AND BRIDGE STREET / TEL: 01799 524002
MON-THU: *9am-3pm;* FRI: *9am-1pm;* SAT-SUN: *10am-4pm*
THE FRY ART GALLERY
CASTLE STREET, SAFFRON WALDEN CB10 1BD / TEL: 01799 513779
FIRST SUNDAY IN APRIL TO LAST SUNDAY IN OCTOBER, TUE, THU, FRI: *2pm-5pm;* SAT: *11am-5pm;* SUN/BANK HOLIDAY: *2.15pm-5pm*
THE KINGS ARMS
10 MARKET HILL, SAFFRON WALDEN CB10 1HQ / TEL: 01799 522768
DAILY: *12noon-late*

ST LEONARDS-ON-SEA

HASTINGS' SMALLER, SCRUFFIER NEIGHBOUR, the two are quite close enough to see in a single day — just 15 or so minutes' walk from one to the other along the seafront. The town's great cultural sites are in plain view, the first almost as you exit the station. On Kings Road, about midway, look up to see recently uncovered, signwriting, beautiful in its own right and thought to be the work of Robert Tressell, author of The Ragged Trousered Philanthropists. The other must-see is the art deco **MARINE COURT**, looking more like an ocean liner than the block of flats it is. At its ground level is **HALFMAN! HALFBURGER!** — for which no explanation is needed, save to say that in this instance single-mindedness pays off. **ST CLEMENTS** is a less frenetic option, serving excellent food in the Modern British idiom. It shares an interior door with **THE HORSE AND GROOM**, a proper pub with horseshoe bar and the burble of conversation. Should ale of a crafty nature be what you require, **THE ST LEONARD** is a fine option. The antique shops of Norman Road are of variable quality but worth browsing if you have the patience. **KINO-TEATR** should satisfy most cravings — arthouse cinema, art gallery and restaurant, all housed in a building returned to its original purpose after years as a builders' merchant.

....

CHARING CROSS TO ST LEONARDS WARRIOR
SQUARE / **JOURNEY TIME** 89 minutes
HALFMAN! HALFBURGER!
7 MARINE COURT, ST LEONARDS TN38 0DX /
TEL: 01424 552332
TUE-SAT: *12noon-10pm*; SUN: *12noon-8pm*
ST CLEMENTS
3 MERCATORIA, ST LEONARDS TN38 0EB
TEL: 01424 200355
TUE-FRI: *12noon-3pm & 6pm-9pm*;
SAT: *12noon-3pm & 6pm-11pm (two sittings)*
THE HORSE AND GROOM
4 MERCATORIA, ST LEONARDS TN38 0EB /
MON-SAT: *11am-11pm*; SUN: *12noon-10.30pm*
THE ST LEONARD
16-18 LONDON ROAD, ST LEONARDS
TN37 6AN / TEL: 01424 272332
WED-SAT: *5pm-11pm*; SUN: *3pm-9pm*
KINO-TEATR
43-49 NORMAN ROAD, ST LEONARDS TN38
0EQ / TEL: 01424 457830

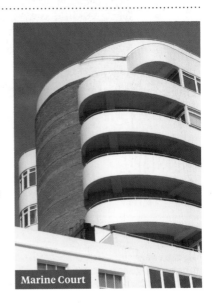

Marine Court

WHITSTABLE

WE HAVE YET TO MEET SOMEONE impervious to the charms of this little fishing town, with its fishermen's huts, pebble beach, small shops, restaurants and harbour, still in use by the town's fleet. The harbour is also site of a market for fresh fish and seafood, with barbecues in summer and, of course, Whitstable oysters, enjoyed far and wide but best eaten at source. Try also **WHEELERS OYSTER BAR**, a snug little place with a counter in front and tiny room in the back (booking advised). A more formal option is **THE WHITSTABLE OYSTER COMPANY**, which has the added attraction of seafront views. It is no surprise to find fish

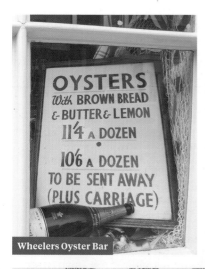

Wheelers Oyster Bar

JoJo's Meze, Meat & Fish

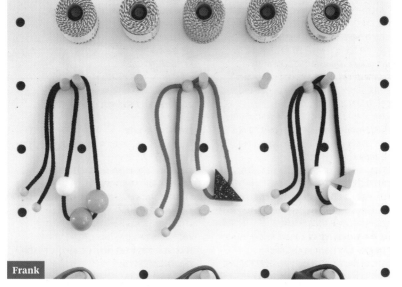

Frank

(Top right) JoJo's /Swooning Dad Design

and chips on offer everywhere, amid stiff competition, family-run **VC JONES** is pick of the bunch. **JOJO'S MEZE, MEAT & FISH RESTAURANT** has a name that requires little extra description, except to say that this attractively minimal beach-side spot does what it states with great aplomb, and that booking ahead is advised. **THE OLD NEPTUNE** pub is right on the beach, a spot for picture-postcard sunsets. On Harbour Street, try **FRANK** for a good selection of British prints, stationery, ceramics and independent magazines; **THE SUGAR BOY** for old-fashioned sweets such as bon bons, sours and acid drops, dispensed from the jar, just as they should be; **PEARL & HEMINGWAY** also recalls a different era in its superior range of vintage clothing for men and women. **VALENTINES VINTAGE**, close to the station has midcentury furniture and homewares, and a shop dog that you'll want to take home with you.

. . . .

ST PANCRAS INTERNATIONAL TO WHITSTABLE /
JOURNEY TIME APPROX 75 MINUTES
VICTORIA TO WHITSTABLE /
JOURNEY TIME APPROX 85 MINUTES
WHEELERS OYSTER BAR
8 HIGH STREET, WHITSTABLE CT5 1BQ /
TEL: 01227 273311
MON-TUE: *10.30am-9pm;*
THU: *10.15am-9pm;* FRI: *10.15am-9.30pm;*
SAT: *10am-10pm;* SUN: *11.30am-9pm*
THE WHITSTABLE OYSTER COMPANY
HORSEBRIDGE, WHITSTABLE CT5 1BU /
TEL: 01227 276 856
MON-THU: *12noon-2.30pm & 6.30pm-9pm;*
FRI: *12noon-2.30pm & 6.30pm-9.30pm;*
SAT: *12noon-9.45pm;* SUN: *12noon-8.30pm*
VC JONES
25 HARBOUR STREET, WHITSTABLE CT5 1AH /
TEL: 01227 272703
TUE-SAT: *11.30am-8pm;* SUN: *12noon-8pm (summer) & 12noon-5pm (winter);* BANK
HOLIDAY MON: *11.30am-8pm*
JOJO'S MEZE, MEAT & FISH RESTAURANT
2 HERNE BAY ROAD, TANKERTON,
WHITSTABLE CT5 2LQ / TEL: 01227 274591
THU-SAT: *12.30pm-3pm & 6.30pm-11pm;*

SUN: *12.30pm-3pm;* WED: *6.30pm-11pm (half-term and school holidays only)*
COFFEE SHOP, TUE-SUN: *9am-5pm*
THE OLD NEPTUNE
MARINE TERRACE, ISLAND WALL,
WHITSTABLE CT5 1EJ / TEL: 01227 272262
SUN-THU: *12noon-10.30pm;* FRI-SAT: *12noon-11.30pm*
FRANK
65 HARBOUR STREET, WHITSTABLE CT5 1AG
/ TEL: 01227 262500
MON, WED-FRI: 10.30AM-5PM;
SAT: *10.30am-6pm;* SUN: *11am-5pm*
OPEN SEVEN DAYS DURING SCHOOL
HOLIDAYS
THE SUGAR BOY
23 HARBOUR STREET, WHITSTABLE CT5 1AH /
TEL: 01227 282202
MON-SAT: *10am-5pm;* SUN: *11am-4pm*
PEARL & HEMINGWAY
14 HARBOUR STREET, WHITSTABLE CT5 1AQ /
TEL: 01227 770000
THU-MON: *11am-5pm*
VALENTINES VINTAGE
21 OXFORD STREET, WHITSTABLE CT5 1DB /
TEL: 01227 281224
MON-SAT: *10am-5.30pm;* SUN: *11am-4pm*

90-120 MINUTES

ARUNDEL CASTLE

BETH CHATTO GARDENS

DE LA WARR PAVILLION

DEAL

EASTBOURNE

HASTINGS

MARGATE

NEW FOREST

PALLANT HOUSE GALLERY

POWELL-COTTON MUSEUM / QUEX HOUSE

STROUD

WALTON-ON-THE-NAZE / FRINTON-ON-SEA

WEST MERSEA

ARUNDEL CASTLE

ARCHITECTURAL HISTORIANS HAVE A TENDENCY TO BE SNIFFY about this castle, largely because of substantial alterations over the past 900 years, yet to the untrained eye it appears picture perfect. Entire sections of the castle — such as the Norman keep — are genuinely old, and views across the South Downs from the battlements are dizzying and beautiful. It takes a few hours to explore the gardens and grounds fully, but allow time to wander in the pretty town, which has a good second hand bookshop and plenty of places to pick up a snack to enjoy on the banks of the River Arun.

ARUNDEL, West Sussex BN18 9AB / TEL: 01903 882173
SEASONAL OPENING, *from Good Friday to last Sunday in October*
TUE-SUN (EASTER MONDAY, MAY BANK HOLIDAY MONDAYS & AUGUST MONDAYS): *10am-5pm (last admission 4pm)*
VICTORIA TO ARUNDEL, *approx 10 minute walk* / **JOURNEY TIME** 90 minutes

BETH CHATTO GARDENS

DEVELOPED OVER THE LAST HALF CENTURY from a marshy wasteland, the gardens are both lovely to walk in and a showcase for the talents of nonagenarian Beth Chatto, who continues to oversee their development. These are not precise, formal plantings, they're something more beguiling and romantic — dense, cushion-like, lush. There are around 2,000 plants in total, arranged in five settings: Scree and Gravel (for drought resistant species), Water, Reservoir, Woodland. This is a place with the capacity to inspire, handy then that there's an attached nursery full of plants to take home. A tea room serves homemade light meals, with views of the garden.

....

ELMSTEAD MARKET, COLCHESTER, ESSEX CO7 7DB / TEL: 01206 822007
MARCH-OCTOBER, MON-SAT: *9am-5pm*; SUN: *10am-5pm*
NOVEMBER-FEBRUARY, MON-SAT: *9am-4pm*; SUN: *10am-4pm*
LIVERPOOL STREET TO COLCHESTER TOWN *(trains to Colchester are more frequent but require a change), approx 30 minute bus ride* / **JOURNEY TIME** 100 MINUTES

DE LA WARR PAVILION

AN EXCELLENT ARTS CENTRE, with three galleries and a large auditorium. Exhibitions are frequently worth a daytrip, with plenty of big names represented, among them Bridget Riley, Otto Dix and Ivan Chermayeff. Even if nothing appeals, the space is magnificent, as perfect a 1930s structure as exists in this country. The café and restaurant have splendid sea views and the roof terrace is wonderful on a sunny day.

MARINA, BEXHILL-ON-SEA, EAST SUSSEX TN40 1DP / TEL: 01424 229111
SUMMER OPENING TIMES (FROM 27 MARCH) DAILY (AND BANK HOLIDAYS): *10am-6pm;*
WINTER OPENING TIMES: *10am-5pm, closed Christmas Day*
VICTORIA TO BEXHILL, *approx 10 minute walk* / **JOURNEY TIME** 120 minutes

Walmer Castle

HUGGING THE SEA FRONT, *the atmospheric old town is a warren of little streets linked by alleyways. In the 18th and 19th centuries many of the pretty houses would have been pubs and brothels, today they're painted in attractive colours, with decorative ships in windows. For a small town, it's bustling with good shopping and food, a mere sampling of which follows.*

ST PANCRAS INTERNATIONAL TO DEAL / **JOURNEY TIME** 100 MINUTES, *change at Ramsgate (until 2017, at which time trains run direct)*

THE BLACK DOUGLAS

Austere, dark-fronted coffee shop that would fit seamlessly into one of the chicer streets of East London but instead has views straight out to sea. Local ingredients are used to make simple and delicious breakfast, lunch and tea.
83 BEACH STREET, DEAL CT14 6JB / TEL: 01304 365486
MON-THU: *9am-5pm;* FRI-SAT: *9am-5pm & 7-10pm;* SUN: *10am-4pm*

FROG AND SCOT

Somewhat utilitarian styling presumably helps keep prices keen for excellent brasserie-style food — bavette steak, confit duck, cassoulet — with plenty of options for appetites large and small. Booking advised.
86 HIGH STREET, DEAL CT14 6EG / TEL: 01304 379444
WED-THU: *6.30pm-11pm;* FRI-SUN: *12noon-11pm*

LE PINARDIER

Wine shop and (evening) bar. Pick up something to crack open on the beach.
102 HIGH STREET, DEAL CT14 6EE / TEL: 01304 372788
WED-THU: *5pm-11pm;* FRI: *12noon-11pm;* SAT: *11am-11pm;* SUN: *12noon-8pm*

POPPY'S KITCHEN

Tasty snacking options for when beetroot, quinoa, avocado and spinach seem like a better idea than fish and chips.
119 HIGH STREET, DEAL CT14 6BB / TEL: 01304 371719
MON-SAT: *9am-5.30pm;* SUN: *10am-3pm*

Le Pinardier

THE SHIP INN

Cosy, woody and gently battered, one almost wishes for a storm that would necessitate holing up for an afternoon in this cabin-like space. If the sun's out, all is not lost, there's a garden to enjoy too. Probably not a wise choice as the first stop, you may never leave.
141 MIDDLE STREET, DEAL CT14 6JZ / TEL: 01304 372222
MON-SAT: *11am-12midnight;* SUN: *12noon-12midnight*

DELPIERRE ANTIQUES

No fancy French furniture here, instead a very good selection of vintage clothes and accessories for women and men, all in excellent condition.
132 HIGH STREET, DEAL CT14 6BE / TEL: 01304 370200
THU-SAT: *10.30am-4.30pm*

MILEAGE VINTAGE HOME & TEA STATION

Sensible pricing and varied stock is the signature of this friendly vintage shop. There are items big and small, from mugs and bread bins to fairground signs and kitchen dressers. A tea shop in the back is a cheerful spot to refuel.

156 HIGH STREET, DEAL CT14 6BG /
TEL: 01304 363311
MON-TUE: *11am-5pm;* THU-FRI: *11am-5pm;*
SAT: *10am-5pm*

SMUGGLERS RECORDS

Every town should have an independent record shop, and this one (an outgrowth of the label of the same name) fits the bill very well indeed. Making it even more enticing, Smugglers also sells bottles and cans of craft beer.

7 KING STREET, DEAL CT14 6HU /
TEL: 01304 362368
MON-WED: *9am-5pm;* THU-SAT: *9am-8pm;*
SUN: *9am-3pm*

DEAL CASTLE AND WALMER CASTLE

Technically fortifications rather than castles, both Deal and Walmer are part of a sequence of Device Forts built as coastal defences by Henry VIII in the first half of the 16th century. Deal Castle is squat and only sparsely ornamented, it's surprising to visit a historic building left as plain and functional as this. A mile or so to the west — a bracing walk along the coastal path — is Walmer Castle, a more lavish affair and the rural retreat for the Lord Warden of the Cinque Ports, a post held by William Pitt the Younger, the Duke of Wellington and Winston Churchill. Collections associated with their occupancies are on display, and there are gardens to enjoy too.

DEAL CASTLE. MARINE ROAD, DEAL
CT14 7BA / TEL: 03703 331181
SEASONAL OPENING, call for details
WALMER CASTLE, KINGSDOWN ROAD,
DEAL CT14 7LJ / TEL: 01304 364288
SEASONAL OPENING, call for details

PIER

Kent's only pier is also the UK's only post-war pier, it's a surprise to see something so modern in so picturesque a setting, and it works all the better for it. A café at the end is a 2008 addition which looks the part but has work to do before it can begin to compete with options elsewhere.

SEASONAL OPENING

Mileage

EASTBOURNE

BETWEEN THE CHALKY MASS OF THE SOUTH DOWNS *and chilly Channel waters, some 100,000 people make their home, and it's easy to see why. Pebbled beach stretches four miles east to west and the seafront is largely unchanged since Victorian times, thanks to local landowner The Duke of Devonshire's unwillingness to allow the development of shops.*

VICTORIA TO EASTBOURNE / **JOURNEY TIME** 95 MINUTES

THINGS TO SEE AND DO

BEACHY HEAD

A 13X Tourist Trail bus will take you to this chalk headland, from which are magnificent views across the coastline and out to sea. The clifftop is a notorious suicide spot, now patrolled by Beachy Head Chaplaincy Team.

EASTBOURNE REDOUBT

Circular brick fortress built as defence from the threat of invasion during the Napoleonic wars, and used on and off by the army until World War Two. It's now a military museum, with keen emphasis on keeping children entertained. The parade ground and gun platform are free to visit.

ROYAL PARADE, EASTBOURNE BN22 7AQ / TEL: 01323 410300
SEASONAL OPENING, call for details

Beachy Head

HOW WE LIVED THEN

Using items acquired over many decades of collecting, this is a history of British domestic life from the 1800s to World War Two. Presented in a cheerfully non-academic approach as a series of shops and rooms arranged over four floors. At the time of writing the owners are looking for a buyer.

20 CORNFIELD TERRACE, EASTBOURNE BN21 4NS / TEL: 01323 737143
SEASONAL OPENING, call for details

PIER

Restored after a fire in 2014, the town's pier seems to be flourishing as it heads to its 150th anniversary. At the far end, above what was a theatre, is the camera obscura, a feature of the Victorian original that was reinstated early this century.

TOWNER GALLERY

Contemporary art gallery in a purpose-built space that replaces the Georgian house it had occupied since the 1920s. Towner holds diverse temporary exhibits along with an impressive permanent collection, notable for a number of works by Sussex native Eric Ravilious (1903-1942) and the gallery's archive.
The top floor café has lovely views across town.

DEVONSHIRE PARK, COLLEGE ROAD, EASTBOURNE BN21 4JJ / TEL: 01323 434670
TUE-SUN: *10am-5pm*

SHOPS

CAMILLA'S BOOKSHOP

A shop so abundant in its wares that bibliophiles may anxiously check the time of the latest return train on entering. Enormous quantity — an estimated million — is matched by tremendous variety. If a suitcase or steamer trunk is needed for your purchases, the Little Chelsea Antiques Emporium over the road may be able to help.

57 GROVE ROAD, EASTBOURNE BN21 4TX /
TEL: 01323 736001
MON-SAT: *10am-5.30pm*

EMMA MASON

An excellent range of 20th century and modern original prints by British artists. There's a lot to take in, including some big names — Robert Tavener, Geoffrey Elliott, David Gentleman, Walter Hoyle. There's also a good range of greetings cards.

3 CORNFIELD TERRACE, EASTBOURNE
BN21 4NN / TEL: 01323 727545
THU-SAT: *10am-5pm*

FRANÇOIS

Old postcards, photographs, books and assorted ephemera are the stock in trade of the eponymous François. Prices are reasonable, but the treasure hunt aspect of this agreeably chaotic shop is dangerously tempting.

26 SOUTH STREET, EASTBOURNE BN21 4XB /
TEL: 01323 644464
TUE, SAT: *10am-5pm*

PLACES TO EAT AND DRINK

FUSCIARDI'S

Serving gelato since 1967, on a sunny day it's worth braving crowds for.

30 MARINE PARADE, EASTBOURNE
BN22 7AY / TEL: 01323 722128
SUN-FRI: *9am-7pm;* SAT: *9am-8pm*

NOTARIANNI'S MILK BAR & RESTAURANT

A rare and wonderful Anglo-Italian survivor. The fascia is magnificent, with its original 1940s pale grey tiles in an elongated honeycomb shape. The interior is not so untouched (lava lamps being one questionable addition), but egg and chips followed by a scoop of gelato will set you up, no matter how bracing it may be outside.

201-203 TERMINUS ROAD, EASTBOURNE
BN21 3DH / TEL: 01323 723332
DAILY: *9am-9pm*

HASTINGS

East Hill Lift

SMALL ENOUGH TO FEEL MANAGEABLE *and large enough to be interesting, this town enjoys the benefits that come from an influx of energetic and relatively moneyed migrants from London and other parts of the south east.*

CHARING CROSS TO HASTINGS / **JOURNEY TIME** 95 minutes

THINGS TO SEE AND DO

EAST AND WEST HILL LIFTS

The west lift has in its favour original wooden Victorian carriages and the Smugglers' Caves. The east has the more spectacular ascent and views, and access to Hastings Country Park.

EAST HILL, ROCK-A-NORE ROAD, HASTINGS TN34 3DW

WEST HILL, GEORGE STREET, HASTINGS TN34 3EG

OPEN APRIL-SEPTEMBER, DAILY: *10am-5.30pm*; OCTOBER-MARCH, DAILY: *11am-4pm*

HASTINGS ADVENTURE GOLF

Three 18-hole miniature golf courses, enough to keep even the most ardent fan satisfied. Small wonder that the World Crazy Golf Championships is held here every October.

PELHAM PLACE, HASTINGS TN34 3AJ

APRIL-OCTOBER, DAILY: *9am-10pm*

NOVEMBER-MARCH, MON-FRI: *10am-4pm*; SAT-SUN: *10am-5pm*

HASTINGS MUSEUM

An eclectic collection of objects and paintings related to the town and its residents, such as Archie Belaney, an early conservationist who styled himself as a Native American, adopting the name Grey Owl.

JOHN'S PLACE, BOHEMIA ROAD, HASTINGS TN34 1ET / TEL: 01424 451052

APRIL-OCTOBER, TUE-SAT: *10am-5pm*; SUN: *12noon-5pm*

NOVEMBER-MARCH, TUE-SAT: *10am-4pm*; SUN: *12noon-4pm*

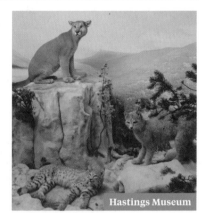
Hastings Museum

JERWOOD GALLERY

A mix of old-fashioned seaside charm and 21st-century regeneration is key to Hastings' appeal. Those elements are most apparent here, in the juxtaposition of The Stade, seafront home to the town's fishing fleet, its nets and equipment stored in double-height, tarred and weatherboarded huts, and the Jerwood Gallery (opened 2012), with a black exterior echoing the tarred finish of its neighbours. British art of the early and mid 20th century is its focus, with works by Walter Sickert, Stanley Spencer, Augustus John, John Bratby and Quentin Blake.

ROCK-A-NORE ROAD, HASTINGS TN34 3DW / TEL: 01424 728377

TUE-SUN: *11am-5pm*; BANK HOLIDAY MON: *11am-5pm*

SHOPS

A G HENDY & CO HOME STORE

Taking a yearning for a pre-digital era to an extreme that lies somewhere between art, commerce and parody, photographer, chef and food stylist Alastair Hendy has meticulously recreated a 19th-century hardware shop, selling enamelware, candles, brushes, soap and other such items, all of which are exquisitely displayed across three floors. An attached restaurant serves simple, delicious lunch on weekends, although the prices are noticeably contemporary.

36 HIGH STREET, HASTINGS TN34 3ER / TEL: 01424 447171
TUE-SUN: *11am-5.30pm*; BANK HOLIDAY MON: *11am-5.30pm*

THE OLD TOWN

This is the area to begin any search for antiques or vintage items. Notable among many are Butler's Emporium, with its magnificent shopfront and the ever-rewarding Robert's Rummage.

ROBERT'S RUMMAGE, 70-71 GEORGE STREET, HASTINGS TN34 3EE/TEL: 01424 420425
MON-SAT: *10am-5pm*; SUN: *11am-5pm*

WOW AND FLUTTER

Unusually well organised new and used secondhand record and book shop. There's also coffee and tea available.

19 CLAREMONT, HASTINGS TN34 1HA / TEL: 01424 439859
WED-SAT: *11am-5pm*

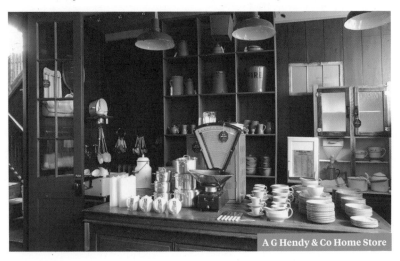
A G Hendy & Co Home Store

PLACES TO EAT AND DRINK

MAGGIE'S (AND MORE)

For impeccable fish and chips, Maggie's comes highly recommended, in fact it's wise to book ahead. The **BLUE DOLPHIN** and **THE NEPTUNE** are also exemplary in every way.

MAGGIES, FISHMARKET ROAD, HASTINGS TN34 3DW / TEL: 01424 430205
MON-SAT: *12noon-2pm*
THE BLUE DOLPHIN, 61B HIGH STREET, TN34 3EJ / TEL: 01424 532869
DAILY: *12noon-10pm*
THE NEPTUNE, 4-6 PLEASANT ROW, HASTINGS TN34 3AS /
TEL: 01424 714638
SUN-FRI: *11.30am-8pm*; SAT: *11.30am-9pm*

ROCK-A-NORE KITCHEN

The freshest fish and seafood, landed just paces away, is served in a weatherboarded hut that blends in with the neighbouring net stores. Delicious and unpretentious cooking.

23A ROCK-A-NORE ROAD, HASTINGS TN34 3DW / TEL: 01424 433764
THU-SAT: *12.30pm-3.30pm & 7pm-10pm*; SUN: *12.30pm-3.30pm*

TUSH & PAT'S FISHERMEN'S ROLLS

A rare example of native English street food. There's just one item on the menu, the Fisherman's Roll, two pieces of fresh pan-fried fish served on a soft roll. At £2.80, it's cheap too.

ROCK-A-NORE ROAD, HASTINGS TN34 /
TEL: 01424 451111
SEASONAL OPENING, call for details

First In Last Out

DI POLA'S

If the sun shows even a willingness to shine, that's a good enough reason to sample a wonderful selection of ices.

14 MARINE PARADE, HASTINGS TN34 3AH /
TEL: 01424 203666
SEASONAL OPENING, call for details

THE DOLPHIN INN

An unaffected local. Good ales, friendly staff and an excellent location make this the pick of the bunch.

11-12 ROCK-A-NORE ROAD, HASTINGS TN34 3DW / TEL: 01424 431197
DAILY: *11am-11pm*

FIRST IN LAST OUT

Good food, an open fire and beer brewed in their own brewery just up the road are all part of FILO's appeal. Also in its favour: no music or loud gaming machines, making it ideal for chatting or reading.

14-15 HIGH STREET, HASTINGS TN34 3EY /
TEL: 01424 425079
MON-SAT: *12noon-11.30pm*; SUN: *12noon-11pm*

Scenic Railway, Dreamland

IN RECENT YEARS *Margate has become such a staple of Sunday supplement articles about the flight from London that it's a surprise to emerge from the station into a seaside town seemingly little different to any other: sandy beach, faded grandeur, menacing seagulls. Even on weekends it can still appear quiet, but things are happening and listed below are some of the most appealing.*

ST PANCRAS INTERNATIONAL TO MARGATE / **JOURNEY TIME** 95 MINUTES

THINGS TO SEE AND DO

DREAMLAND

Rescued from dereliction, the country's oldest amusement park has been revived to great effect. It's a little self-consciously retro — an accusation that some might level at much of the town — but if that means bringing back original rides like the bone-rattling 1920s Scenic Railway and 1970s Dodgems, count us in.

MARINE TERRACE, MARGATE CT9 1XJ / TEL: 01843 295887

SEASONAL OPENING, call for details

Dreamland

SHELL GROTTO

If Turner Contemporary represents new Margate and Dreamland the town restored, the Shell Grotto is for the ages. Allegedly discovered while digging for a pond in 1835, the date at least seems true enough. Whether created by druids or a bored eccentric, the place is undeniably peculiar: a network of tunnels and caves, its walls entirely covered in patterns formed by a total of 4.6 million shells. There were once seances held in these chambers, but now that nondescript houses have sprouted at street level, in some ways it's weirder than ever.

GROTTO HILL, MARGATE CT9 2BU / TEL: 01843 220008

SEASONAL OPENING, call for details

Turner Contemporary

TURNER CONTEMPORARY

Frequently cited as the single largest factor in Margate's regeneration, there's no denying the gallery's crowd-pulling power. Huge windows look directly out to sea, with particularly dramatic views from the first floor. There's no permanent collection but temporary exhibitions have featured big names, among them Jeremy Deller, Grayson Perry and one JMW Turner.

RENDEZVOUS, MARGATE CT9 1HG / TEL: 01843 233000

TUE-SUN: *10am-6pm*

SHOPS

BREUER & DAWSON

Along with sea air and contemporary art, the town's other great lure is shopping for clothes and furniture from past decades. In charming premises with a hand-painted fascia redolent of sterner times, Breuer & Dawson sell high quality vintage clothing: benchmade brogues, Guernsey sweaters, 1980s brothel creepers, university scarves, cycle tops, waxed cotton jackets and more.

7 KING STREET, MARGATE CT9 1DD /
TEL: 01843 225299
TUE-SUN: *11am-5pm*

Breuer & Dawson

HAECKELS

Pungent local seaweed is turned into fragrant scents, candles and grooming products at this aromatic, atmospheric shop and laboratory. Located at the west end of town, it's a little past the Turner, in Cliftonville, an area rapidly sprouting new shops and places to eat, notably on Northdown Road.

18 CLIFF TERRACE, MARGATE CT9 1RU /
TEL: 07955 559205
DAILY: *10.30am-5pm*

MARGATE OLD TOWN

Rather than list every shop worth visiting, our advice is to wander these few streets which are home to vintage clothiers, furniture shops, photography gallery and bookshop **VORTIGERN**, and several places to eat.

R G SCOTT'S FURNITURE MART / JUNK DELUXE

Not far from the Shell Grotto is another must-see, Scott's is more of a warehouse than a shop, jammed with used furniture and items for anyone with a restoration project. Here's where to find hinges, knobs and knockers, table legs, sash weights, tiles, railings, loo roll holders, newel posts and more.

Deeper into the same building is Junk Deluxe, which specialises in articles of mid to late 20th century furniture and homeware, much of it Continental in origin.

THE OLD ICEWORKS, BATH PLACE, MARGATE
CT9 2BN / TEL: 07963 892041;
07952 884117
THU-SAT: *9.30am-1pm & 2pm-5pm* (CLOSED
BANK HOLIDAYS)

PLACES TO EAT AND DRINK

CHEESY TIGER / HARBOUR ARMS

Winter can be brutal in this windy town, but it's always snug inside these two little boltholes on the harbour wall. Cheesy Tiger is a lively, bohemian take on a wine bar, with a miniscule open kitchen. The Harbour Arms is a true micro pub. Cosy as they are, it's even better when you can sit outside.

UNITS 7 & 8 HARBOUR ARM, MARGATE CT9 1JD / TEL: 01843 448550 (Cheesy Tiger)/07776 183273 (Harbour Arms)
SEASONAL OPENING/DAILY: *11.30am-11.30pm*

GB PIZZA

Delicate, thin and crispy pizzas with toppings to appeal to all, using locally sourced ingredients where possible. Canteen-style tables fill up quickly on sunny weekends, so we suggest reserving seats.

14A MARINE DRIVE, MARGATE CT9 1DH / TEL: 01843 297700
DAILY: *12noon-9pm*

THE LIFEBOAT

If Slow Drink ever takes off like Slow Food, this may be considered ground zero. Staff navigate through the crowd to walls of boxes and casks a few feet away, returning with drinks some time later. The Lifeboat may look like a survivor from Margate's seafaring past, in fact it's an artful refit of a wine bar.

1 MARKET STREET, MARGATE CT9 1EU / TEL: 07837024259
SUN-WED: *12noon-1am;* THU-SAT: *12noon-2am* ("*We may shut early but never before 10pm*")

LONDON TAVERN

A large pub with several rooms, each with a slightly different atmosphere so it's worth a recce before settling down. Decent ale, good food and space to spread out are all points in its favour.

ADDINGTON STREET, MARGATE CT9 1PN / TEL: 01843 499759
TUE-THU: *5pm-11pm;* FRI: *1pm-11pm;* SAT: *12noon-11pm;* SUN: *12noon-9pm*

GB Pizza

NEW FOREST

ACROSS 150 SQUARE MILES are areas of dense woodland, heath, bogs and swathes of coastline. There are the famous roaming ponies, cattle, pigs and deer to admire, historic villages to explore and the Motor Museum at Beaulieu. There's far too much to see here in a single day, but it's possible to cover a lot of ground even in just a few hours using three connecting hop-on hop-off open-top bus routes, or by hiring a bike at Brockenhurst station and setting out on your own.

Book discounted tickets for the bus and other attractions from thenewforesttour.info

WATERLOO TO BROCKENHURST / **JOURNEY TIME** 95 minutes

PALLANT HOUSE GALLERY

NOT JUST ONE OF THE COUNTRY'S BEST COLLECTIONS of British modern art, Pallant House also has an exceptional programme of exhibitions, many of which are well worth travelling for. No matter what's on, the building is a delight, it takes the gallery's original home — a remarkably handsome Queen Anne townhouse — added to which is a bold and uncompromisingly modern wing. Inside it's light, harmonious and tranquil, an ideal setting to enjoy the exhibits and no less good for taking advantage of the restaurant and café. In the summer there's seating amid sculpture displays in the walled courtyard. The excellent shop seals the deal, with a selection of artists' prints and out of print books that sets it apart from most similar enterprises.

. . . .

9 NORTH PALLANT, CHICHESTER, WEST SUSSEX PO19 1TJ / TEL: 01243 774557
TUE-SAT: *10am-5pm;* THU: *10am-8pm;* SUN: *11am-5pm*
VICTORIA TO CHICHESTER, *approx 5 minute walk*
JOURNEY TIME 95 minutes

POWELL-COTTON MUSEUM / QUEX HOUSE

IN AN IRONY COMMON to many early conservationists, Major Percy Horace Gordon Powell-Cotton killed an awful lot of animals, large numbers of which can be seen in this museum's spectacular dioramas which are the equal of any in far better known institutions. Ethnography was another passion, and considerable space is given to collections of weapons, talismen and jewellery gathered over the course of his many expeditions. The museum is an addition to Quex House, a few rooms of which are open to the public, as are the grounds. There's a café near the house but a better option is Quex Barn, by the front gate, with its shop and restaurant — a good choice for picnic supplies or eating in.

....

QUEX PARK, BIRCHINGTON CT7 0BH / TEL: 01843 842168
MUSEUM AND GARDENS, MID-JANUARY-MID-DECEMBER, DAILY: *10am-4.30pm*
QUEX HOUSE, APRIL-OCTOBER, DAILY: *1pm-4pm*
ST PANCRAS INTERNATIONAL TO BIRCHINGTON-ON-SEA, *approx 20 minute walk* /
JOURNEY TIME 110 MINUTES

STROUD

NOWHERE IS THE RULE THAT BEAUTY IS ONLY SKIN DEEP more apparent than in the Cotswolds, where the prettiest towns and villages are frequently the least interesting. By comparison, Stroud is not going to win any beauty contests but as a place for a daytrip it has much to offer. The Saturday **FARMERS' MARKET**, spilling out of the purpose-built Cornhill marketplace in the town centre, is huge and a good place to pick up picnic supplies. Two excellent second-hand bookshops, **R&R** and the more refined **INPRINT**, are also worth adding to any itinerary as are **DUFFLE**, for vintage clothing and mid century furniture, and **TIME AFTER TIME** for a good selection of clothes. The towpath of the **STROUDWATER CANAL**, which links the Thames to the Severn, is an atmospheric vantage point from which to see the beautiful hills and valleys that surround the town. The canal will also take you to the **STROUD BREWERY**, for beer and (after 5pm) pizza. In town, **MEME** is a excellent all-day option for a snack or a drink — with an ethical and local menu. If the thought of making conversation is just too much, the **BLACK BOOK CAFÉ** is also a second hand bookshop, where paperbacks cost less than a cup of coffee. For classic gastropub, **BISLEY HOUSE** is a reliable option. For the more adventurous, open country is just minutes away (a good source of routes is strollinginstrouddistrict.org), with **THE WOOLPACK** in Slad, of Laurie Lee fame, only about 45 minutes away.

Meme

PADDINGTON TO STROUD /
JOURNEY TIME 90 minutes
STROUD FARMERS' MARKET
CORNHILL MARKET PLACE, STROUD GL5 2HH
SAT: *9am-2pm*
R&R BOOKS
NELSON STREET, STROUD GL5 2HL /
TEL: 01453 755788
MON-SAT: *10am-5.30pm*
INPRINT
31 HIGH STREET, STROUD GL5 1AJ /
TEL: 01453 759731
TUE-SAT: *10am-5pm*
DUFFLE VINTAGE OUTFITTERS
2 JOHN STREET, STROUD GL5 2HE /
TEL: 01453 758394
MON-SAT: *10am-7pm*; SUN: *10am-6pm*
TIME AFTER TIME
30 HIGH STREET, STROUD GL5 1AJ
MON-FRI: *10am-5pm*; SAT: *9am-5.30pm*
STROUD BREWERY
UNIT 11 LONDON ROAD, THRUPP, GL5 2BU /
TEL: 01453 887122

THU: *5pm-11pm*: FRI-SAT: *3pm-11pm*
MEME
16 GEORGE STREET, STROUD GL5 3DY /
TEL: 01453 759593
TUE-WED: *10am-5pm*;
THU: *10am-11.30pm*; FRI: *10am-1am*;
SAT: *9.30am-1am*
BLACK BOOK CAFÉ
UNIT 2, NELSON STREET, STROUD GL5 2HL /
TEL: 01453 764509
MON-SAT: *9am-4pm*; SUN: *10am-2pm*
BISLEY HOUSE
MIDDLE STREET, STROUD GL5 1DZ /
TEL: 01453 751 328
WED-FRI: *4pm-11pm (food served 6pm-9pm)*;
SAT-SUN: *11am-11pm (food served 12noon-3pm & 6pm-9pm)*
THE WOOLPACK INN
SLAD ROAD, STROUD GL6 7QA /
TEL: 01452 813429
MON-SUN: *12noon-12midnight*
FOOD, MON-SAT: *12noon-3pm & 6pm-9pm*;
SUN: *12noon-4pm*

WALTON-ON-THE-NAZE / FRINTON-ON-SEA

IT SHOULD TAKE NO MORE THAN FIVE MINUTES to walk from the station to the beach, a little longer if you choose to stop at **YATES** for fish and chips. After which all you need do is find some space on this quite magnificent stretch of sand and enjoy the view. Those in search of more entertainment need look no further than **WALTON PIER**, Britain's third longest, equipped with a slightly rough around the edges amusement park. West of the pier, about 20 minutes' walk, is the 86 feet tall **NAZE TOWER**. Built in 1721 as a marker for ships approaching Harwich harbour, it's now a museum and gallery, but is best enjoyed as a viewing platform from which to gaze out at many miles of land and sea. Set out in the other direction for **FRINTON-ON-SEA**, about half an hour away, well equipped with yet more lovely beaches, Deco-esque architecture, charity shops and the unmistakeable whiff of God's waiting room.

LIVERPOOL STREET TO WALTON-ON-THE-NAZE OR FRINTON-ON-SEA *(change at Thorpe-Le-Soken)* / **JOURNEY TIME** 95 minutes

WEST MERSEA

ANCIENT ROMANS WOULD COME HERE TO ESCAPE the hurly-burly of city life in nearby Colchester and today it still serves much the same purpose. It feels blissfully remote, all the more so at high tide when the causeway floods and, true to its name, Mersea Island is cut off from the mainland for a few hours. West Mersea is the more populated half of the island, well appointed for the day-tripper. Traditional huts line the sand and pebble beach which in summer has water just about warm enough to bathe in, and there's a jetty from which to do a bit of crabbing and just maybe spot some seals.

Perhaps it's the effect of the sea air on appetites, but food seems to taste particularly good here. **THE COMPANY SHED** may be worth the trip alone, the sort of bare bones place you'd like to keep as your own secret. Plaudits from chefs and critics mean that long queues are likely at peak times, but happily the place is still as basic as the name suggests. Just a waddle away are **THE COAST INN** and **WEST MERSEA OYSTER BAR** — both worthy rivals to The Company Shed, a little more slick in presentation and with outside seating giving views of the estuary.

LIVERPOOL STREET TO COLCHESTER TOWN *(change at Colchester), approx 35 minute bus ride* / **JOURNEY TIME** 110 MINUTES

THE COAST INN
108 COAST ROAD, WEST MERSEA CO5 8NA / TEL: 01206 383568
MON-FRI: *12noon-3pm & 6pm-9pm;* SAT: *12noon-9pm;* SUN: *12noon-5pm*

THE COMPANY SHED
129 COAST ROAD, WEST MERSEA CO5 8PA / TEL: 01206 382700
TUE-SAT: *9am-4pm;* SUN: *10am-4pm*

WEST MERSEA OYSTER BAR
COAST ROAD, WEST MERSEA CO5 8LT / TEL: 01206 381600
SEASONAL OPENING, call for details

INDEX

INDEX BY COUNTY

We couldn't have done this without really trying.

Thank you to the many people who gave us suggestions and assisted us with this book, notable among them are Jonathan Brooker, Elizabeth Cake, Charlie Claridge, Gary Corben, Nadine Davidson, James and Edwina Finlay, Matthew Freedman, Ian Greensmith, Katie Hayes, Gary Headland, Richard Hutt, Peter Knock, Xtina Lamb, Laura Lee, Rich Little, Iain Pitchford, Kevin Younger.

Our gratitude too to all the businesses, organisations and photographers who allowed us to use their images.

Special thanks to Bryan Mayes, Brice Beasley.